The
TOWER
of the FLOCK

The Christmas Story

DR. CHRISTINE VAN HORN

WESTBOW
PRESS®
A DIVISION OF THOMAS NELSON
& ZONDERVAN

Scripture taken from the Common English Bible®, CEB® Copyright © 2010, 2011 by Common English Bible.™ Used by permission. All rights reserved worldwide. The "CEB" and "Common English Bible" trademarks are registered in the United States Patent and Trademark Office by Common English Bible. Use of either trademark requires the permission of Common English Bible.

Scripture quotations marked (CEV) are from the Contemporary English Version Copyright © 1991, 1992, 1995 by American Bible Society. Used by Permission.

Scripture taken from the New King James Version®. Copyright © 1982 by Thomas Nelson. Used by permission. All rights reserved.

Scripture quotations marked (NIV) are taken from the Holy Bible, New International Version®, NIV®. Copyright © 1973, 1978, 1984, 2011 by Biblica, Inc.™ Used by permission of Zondervan. All rights reserved worldwide. www.zondervan.com The "NIV" and "New International Version" are trademarks registered in the United States Patent and Trademark Office by Biblica, Inc.™

Scripture quotations are taken from the Holy Bible, New Living Translation, copyright ©1996, 2004, 2007, 2013, 2015 by Tyndale House Foundation. Used by permission of Tyndale House Publishers, Inc., Carol Stream, Illinois 60188. All rights reserved.

Scripture quotations taken from the Amplified® Bible (AMP), Copyright © 2015 by The Lockman Foundation. Used by permission. www.Lockman.org

Scriptures Taken from the King James Bible.

WestBow Press books may be ordered through booksellers or by contacting:

WestBow Press
A Division of Thomas Nelson & Zondervan
1663 Liberty Drive
Bloomington, IN 47403
www.westbowpress.com
1 (866) 928-1240

ISBN: 978-1-9736-0913-1 (sc)
ISBN: 978-1-9736-0914-8 (e)

Library of Congress Control Number: 2017918420

Print information available on the last page.

WestBow Press rev. date: 12/01/2017

CONTENTS

DEDICATION

I dedicate this book to:

Dr. Robb Thompson, Pastor of Family Harvest Church (FHC) of Tinley Park, IL. You are our beloved Pastor and my pastor, mentor and coach. During our coaching sessions, you encouraged me to press on with this book. Thank you for all you have sown into my life over the past twenty one years.

Pastor John Paledino, Pastor of Harvest Church of Tampa, Florida and former Associate Pastor of FHC in Tinley Park, IL. During your tenure at FHC, you interested me in studying Theology. I made that decision to do so, and eventually received my Bachelors, Masters and Doctorate Degrees in Theology. Pastor John, thank you for leading me into the scholarly study of the Word of God. I owe much of my passion for studying the Word to you. Thank you also for proclaiming God's healing Word over my husband when illness attacked, and being faithful in your visits and calls. You are a trusted man of God and I thank you for all you have sown into the body of Christ, and into my life.

My husband, John, for walking out this teaching with me for years as I studied.

The Rev. Dr. H.E. Van Horn, my husband's Grandfather. You were a well-known minister at churches in Iowa and Oklahoma City, but passed too soon to finish your mission. You wanted a minister in the family to follow after you, and I have the honor of fulfilling that role. After completing this book, we discovered the book *The Life and Times of Jesus the Messiah* by Alfred Edersheim in your library and writings. This book has been so pivotal in my work. It makes me wonder how much of what I have written was known to you – and if the Holy Spirit gave this revelation to me because of you.

INTRODUCTION

Jesus was the Lamb from before the foundation of the world (Rev. 13:8 NLT). He was foreshadowed as a lamb, He lived as a Lamb, He died as THE Lamb and He is the coming King as The Lamb. "Jesus Christ *is* the same yesterday, today, and forever" (Hebrews 13:8). A forever Lamb also had to be born into this world as a Lamb, which was the Lord's revelation to me that started this study.

The Tower of the Flock builds upon my book, *The Lamb Eternal*. This study focuses on Bethlehem were Jesus was born, the Temple flock (where and how they were raised) and Jesus being born as THE Lamb. For this, we return to the Old Testament. This will connect all that we studied in *The Lamb Eternal* with this study's foundational Scriptures of Micah 4:8 and 5:2.

> As for you, watchtower of the flock,
> Stronghold (hill) of Daughter Zion,
> The former dominion will be restored to you;
> Kingship will come to Daughter Jerusalem…
>
> But you, Bethlehem Ephrathah,
> Though you are small among the clans (rulers) of Judah,
> Out of you will come for me
> One who will be ruler over Israel,
> Whose origins are from of old,
> From ancient times. (Micah 4:8; 5:2 NIV)

Luke Chapter 2 is the source for a better understanding of the birth of Jesus, THE Lamb of God. These passages in Luke will be explored later in detail as you read. For now, note the words in italics, as they are key to this study.

> And it came to pass in those days that a decree went out from Caesar Augustus that all the world should be registered. This census first took place while Quirinius was governing Syria. So all went to be registered, everyone to his own city.

> Joseph also went up from Galilee, out of the city of Nazareth, into Judea, to the city of David, which is called Bethlehem, because he was of the house and lineage of David, to be registered with Mary, his betrothed wife, who was with child. So it was, that *while they were there*, the days were completed for her to be delivered. And she brought forth her firstborn Son, and wrapped Him in *swaddling cloths*, and laid Him in a *manger*, because there was *no room* for them in the inn.

> Now there were in the same country *shepherds living out in the fields*, keeping watch over their flock by night. And behold, an angel of the Lord stood before them, and the glory of the Lord shone around them, and they were greatly afraid. Then the angel said to them, "Do not be afraid, for behold, I bring you good tidings of great joy which will be to all people. For there *is born* to you this day in the city of David a Savior, who is Christ the Lord. And this will be *the sign* to you: You will find a Babe *wrapped in swaddling cloths, lying in a manger.*" And suddenly there was with the angel a multitude of the heavenly host praising God and saying: "Glory to God in the highest, And on earth peace, goodwill toward men!"

> So it was, when the angels had gone away from them into heaven that the shepherds said to one another, "Let us now go to Bethlehem and see this thing that has come to pass, *which the Lord has made known to us.*" And *they came with haste* and found

Mary and Joseph, and the Babe *lying in a manger.* Now when they had seen Him, *they made widely known the saying which was told them concerning this Child.* And all those who heard it marveled at those things which were told them by the shepherds. But Mary kept all these things and pondered them in her heart. Then the shepherds returned, glorifying and praising God for all the things that they had heard and seen, as it was told them. (Luke 2:1–20 NKJV; author's emphasis)

The Tower of the Flock is a continuation of the "one story" of Jesus, THE Lamb of God. I invite you to join it with me.

PROLOGUE

Why write this book? Why is the information provided here so important? What is it about the birth of Jesus that is such a powerful revelation? How does the location, the timing and the background of His birth affect us? The simple answer is that His Birth is the pivotal point in the entirety of human history. Studying this event provides us with insight into the precision of God's Word, His complete plan for the redemption of mankind, and the depth and comprehensiveness of the actions that led to the birth of Jesus, His death and His resurrection.

The book *The Lamb Of God* discusses and details how Christ is involved throughout the past and future of the church and the earth, this book takes a careful look at the background behind His birth. What happened? First you must realize that Jesus was not born in a vacuum. God had carefully prepared the soil. The world was ready for the appearance of the Messiah. God had given the prophets the words to predict the coming of the Messiah, His birth, its location and timing, as well as all that He would suffer as the Lamb to redeem mankind. God then left the world in silence, waiting until the time was ripe.

I want to point out to you that the nation of Israel was not located where it was by chance. Ray Vander Laan several times has stated in his series "That The World May Know" that Israel was located in a very precise position so that God could use it's people to influence the world. Israel was placed in a location that straddled the Via Maris and the Kings Highway. These roads were the two major trade routes between Persia and Egypt, between the East and West. Israel was placed there, in a position to spread God's plan throughout the Middle East, Africa and Europe.

Next God created a fire of belief in His people. Approximately 160 years before the birth of Christ, the Maccabees in their rebellion had re-established the Jewish fierceness in defending their faith. Historically the Maccabeean Rebellion is the source of the Jewish holiday of Hanukkah. The result was the purification of the Temple and the strengthening of the Jewish priesthood. The Jews were expecting God to act on their behalf. There were scholars (the Magi) in Persia who had the knowledge bequeathed by Daniel and his prophecies and who were watching for signs in the heavens. Herod had established the grandeur of the second temple, the Romans had created a comprehensive commercial and military road and water network so that His message could spread throughout the world. The Pax Romana (peace of Rome) was established under the Emperor Augustus, so that people, knowledge and beliefs could travel in safety throughout the Roman Empire.

The soil was ready, the fields were prepared, the people were ready. The time was right. It was time for God to begin the most important series of events in human history, and appropriately they began with the angel Gabriel appearing to one of God's priests in His Temple.

So now let's begin the study.

CHAPTER 1

Bethlehem

Jesus' birth in Bethlehem was prophesied in Scriptures. Why was He born in Bethlehem? Because He was of the line of David, and Bethlehem was David's city. The Book of Micah was written 500 years before Jesus' birth, and Micah 5:2 prophesies the birthplace of Jesus. Here are a few versions of this verse to better understand the full context.

> But you, Bethlehem Ephrathah,
> Though you are little among the thousands of Judah,
> Yet out of you shall come forth to Me
> The One to be Ruler in Israel,
> Whose goings forth are from of old,
> From everlasting. (NKJV)

> But thou, Bethlehem Ephratah, though thou be little among the thousands of Judah, yet out of thee shall he come forth unto me that is to be ruler in Israel; whose goings forth have been from of old, from everlasting. (KJV)

> But you, Bethlehem Ephratah, you are little to be among the clans of Judah; [yet] out of you shall One come forth for Me Who is to be Ruler in Israel, Whose goings forth have been from of old, from ancient days (eternity). (AMP)

> And thou Bethlehem Ephrata, art a little one among the thousands of Judah: out of thee shall he come forth unto me that is to be the

ruler in Israel: and his going forth is from the beginning, from the days of eternity. (Douay Rheims 1899 American Edition)

As for you, Bethlehem of Ephrathah,
though you are the least significant
of Judah's forces,
one who is to be a ruler in Israel
on my behalf
will come out from you.
His origin is from remote times,
from ancient days. (Common English Bible)

This verse says that Bethlehem is a small village from the tribe of Judah. It also says that the ruler of Israel will come from here; Who has His origins in the distant past, or from everlasting. This is none other than the Lord Jesus Christ, the Promised One, THE Lamb of God, the Eternal God. This Scripture was fulfilled as told in the Gospel of Luke. "The Savior—yes, the Messiah, the Lord—has been born today in Bethlehem, the city of David!" (Luke 2:11 NLT).

Bethlehem was David's city, and Jesus was of the lineage of David. How did Bethlehem come to be David's city? It came into the lineage of David long before his time. Let us walk back through Scripture to see where this began. The first time we see Bethlehem is with Jacob, the son of Isaac, and his wife Rachel.

JACOB AND RACHEL

After Jacob stole the birthright from his brother Esau and needed to flee for safety, his father Isaac blessed him and sent him on his way. He told Jacob not to marry a Canaanite woman, but to marry one of the daughters of his uncle Laban (his mother's brother) in the land of Paddan-aram. He also told him that he would own the land in which he was now living.

And give you the blessing of Abraham,
To you and your descendants with you,
That you may inherit the land

> In which you are a stranger,
> Which God gave to Abraham. (Genesis 28:4)

Jacob traveled on to Paddan-aram and along the way at Bethel, he had a dream from the Lord. He dreamed that there was a ladder between the earth and heaven and the angels of God were ascending and descending upon it. The Lord spoke to him and said:

> I am the LORD God of Abraham your father and the God of Isaac; the land on which you lie I will give to you and your descendants. Also your descendants shall be as the dust of the earth; you shall spread abroad to the west and the east, to the north and the south; and in you and in your seed all the families of the earth shall be blessed. Behold, I am with you and will keep you wherever you go, and will bring you back to this land; for I will not leave you until I have done what I have spoken to you. (Genesis 28:13–15)

God reaffirmed the blessing of Abraham to him, that his descendants will be many and blessed. He said He would not leave him, but bless him and bring him back to this land. Jacob proclaimed that this place was the house of God and the gate of heaven. When Jacob arrived at Paddan-aram, he went to a well and met Rachel, one of Laban's daughters. She was a shepherdess. In the Strong's Concordance, Rachel's name means "ewe" (Strong 7354). Men, rather than women, were usually shepherds "but Laban apparently had no sons at the time so this was the responsibility of his youngest daughter, Rachel, to shepherd his flock" (Freeman, 1998, 54).

> Now while he was still speaking with them, Rachel came with her father's sheep, for she was a shepherdess. And it came to pass, when Jacob saw Rachel the daughter of Laban his mother's brother, and the sheep of Laban his mother's brother, that Jacob went near and rolled the stone from the well's mouth, and watered the flock of Laban his mother's brother. Then Jacob kissed Rachel, and lifted up his voice and wept. And Jacob told Rachel that he was her father's relative and that he was Rebekah's son. So she ran and told her father. (Genesis 29:9–12)

Jacob became a shepherd of his uncle Laban's flock for 14 years in order to marry Rachel and her sister Leah, who he was tricked into marrying after working for the first seven years. After twenty years, he left to return to the land of his father. He sent messengers to let his brother, Esau, to let him know he was returning. *Along the journey, he wrestled with God and God changed his name to Israel.* And God said, "Your name shall no longer be called Jacob, but Israel; for you have struggled with God and with men, and have prevailed" (Genesis 32:28). He had a peaceful reunion with Esau and dwelt in the land of his fathers. Rachel became the mother of Joseph (who was later sold into slavery in Egypt and became the second in command there) and Benjamin.

Later God directed Jacob to return to Bethel (where he had the vision of the ladder between earth and heaven). He built an altar to God there. They traveled on from Bethel. But when they neared Ephrath, Rachel went into difficult childbirth and she died. But before she died, her midwife told her that she was giving birth to a son. She wanted to name him Ben-Omi but his father named him Benjamin.

> So Rachel died and was buried on the way to *Ephrath (that is, Bethlehem).* And Jacob set a pillar on her grave, which is the pillar of Rachel's grave to this day. Then Israel journeyed and pitched his tent beyond *the tower of Eder.* (Genesis 35:19–21 NKJV; author's emphasis)

A few other translations of Genesis 35:19–21 are shown to provide an enhanced explanation. Please note the words "Bethlehem," "Ephrath," "Migdal-Eder," and "Eder."

> So Rachel died and was buried on the way to *Ephrath (that is, Bethlehem).* Jacob set up a stone monument over Rachel's grave, and it can be seen there to this day. Then Jacob traveled on and camped beyond *Migdal-eder.* (NLT; author's emphasis)

> And Rachel died, and was buried on the way to *Ephrath,* which [is] *Bethlehem.* And Jacob erected a pillar upon her grave: that is the pillar of Rachel's grave to [this] day. And Israel journeyed, and

spread his tent on the other side of *Migdal-Eder*. (Darby; author's emphasis)

This next set of translations of the same verse provides another important component. They show that Eder (Edar) is a tower. This is of utmost importance.

> And Rachel died, and was buried in the way to Ephrath, which is Bethlehem. And Jacob set a pillar upon her grave: that is the pillar of Rachel's grave unto this day. And Israel journeyed, and spread his tent beyond *the tower of Edar*. (KJV; author's emphasis)

> Rachel was buried beside the road to Ephrath, which is also called Bethlehem. Jacob set up a tombstone over her grave, and it is still there. Jacob, also known as Israel, traveled to the south of *Eder Tower*, where he set up camp. (CEV; author's emphasis)

> So Rachel died and was buried on the way to Ephrath (that is, Bethlehem). Jacob set up a marker on her grave; it is the marker at Rachel's grave to this day. Israel set out again and pitched his tent beyond the *Tower of Eder*. (Holman Christian Standard Bible; author's emphasis)

This last translation gives another enhancement. Where the other translations list the Tower of Eder, this version explains that it is a Flock tower. It is from the Douay-Reims translation, the first translation of the Bible into English.

> So Rachel died, and was buried in the highway that leadeth to Ephrata, that is Bethlehem. And Jacob erected a pillar over her sepulcher: this is the pillar of Rachel's monument, to this day. Departing thence, he pitched his tent beyond *the Flock tower*. (Douay–Rheims 1899 American Edition; author's emphasis)

As noted in *The Lamb Eternal*, the Douay-Rheims Bible is important. It was originally translated to English from St. Jerome's Latin Vulgate, which he translated from Hebrew to Latin around 400 A.D. The exact words in the Douay-Rheims are directly tied to Latin, which was directly tied to the original Hebrew. *This means that the specificity of the tower of Eder being called a "Flock tower" carries a lot of weight in it's meaning.*

There are other translations that explain it as a "watchtower." That is also important. To summarize the important content in Genesis 35:19–21:

- Bethlehem is also called Ephrath or Ephrata
- Rachel died outside of Bethlehem after giving birth to Benjamin and was buried there
- Israel (Jacob) pitched his tent beyond Mgdal-Eder (Eder) which was also a tower – the Flock Tower (tower of the flock, tower of Eder, watchtower of the flock)

But the Amplified Version provides yet another understanding that the Tower of Eder was a lookout point used by shepherds.

> So Rachel died and was buried on the way to Ephrath (that is, Bethlehem). Jacob set a pillar (memorial, monument) on her grave; that is the [a]pillar of Rachel's grave to this day. Then Israel (Jacob) journeyed on and pitched his tent on the other side of *the tower of Eder [the lookout point used by shepherds]*. (AMP; author's emphasis)

This means that the tower of Eder was built on a high place overlooking the fields used by the shepherds. This is also key. It was built on the high point in the area. That makes sense because a lookout for the shepherds in the area would have to be on the highest point. It would give the best visual of the sheep and watching for any predators to protect them.

The reason so many translations are inserted here is to bring out the in depth of the meaning. It ties them to our foundation Scriptures of Micah 5:2, 4:8. Rachel, the shepherdess, was buried near Midgal Edar, the tower of the flock, by Bethlehem. *This is the first time that Bethlehem is noted in the Bible.* It is also described as the Tower of the Flock and Migdal Eder. The story on Bethlehem continues…but we will return to this information later.

On another note, Rachel's tomb still exists today, and the Jews visit it as a holy place.

RUTH

Another person from the Old Testament connected with the heritage of Bethlehem is Ruth. You can study her story in the Book of Ruth in the Old Testament. She was the daughter-in-law of Elimelech and Naomi. Elimelech was a man from Bethlehem in Judah, who went to dwell in Moab with his wife, Naomi. They had two sons who married women from Moab. Elimelech and his sons died, leaving the three women. Naomi told the women to return to their families. One did, but the other named Ruth remained with Naomi. Ruth's words to Naomi, and her decision to return to Bethlehem with Naomi, play an important role in the earthly heritage of Jesus. (Note: It is also quoted today as part of marriage ceremonies. My husband and I used it for our wedding).

> Intreat me not to leave thee,
> or to return from following after thee:
> for whither thou goest, I will go;
> and where thou lodgest, I will lodge:
> thy people shall be my people,
> and thy God my God:
> Where thou diest, will I die,
> and there will I be buried:
> the Lord do so to me, and more also,
> if ought but death part thee and me.
> (Ruth 1:16–17 KJV)

Ruth returned with Naomi to her homeland in Bethlehem. Ruth went to glean in the fields for grain for Naomi and herself so they could eat. (Note: gleaning is explained in Leviticus 19:9 and states that when harvesting their fields, the reapers were to leave what had fallen at the corners for the poor and strangers). A man named Boaz saw her and found favor in her. Boaz was from the family of Elimelech. He told her to just glean from his fields and none other. He protected her and provided for her and Naomi.

Boaz told her that he knew what she had done for Naomi, and that the Lord would repay and protect her.

Boaz fed her as she worked the fields, and he commanded his men to purposely let grain fall for her. When Ruth told Naomi whose fields she gleaned, Naomi told her that he was a relative. She continued to live with Naomi and work in the fields of Boaz. One day, Naomi told Ruth to go down to the threshing floor where Boaz was working. She was to lay at his feet when he slept.

Boaz awoke and found her and said that she was a virtuous woman, and that he was a close relative. But there was one relative closer than himself. Since he was a relative, as was this other man, one of them could be a "kinsman redeemer" to Naomi and to Ruth. A kinsman redeemer was the closest family member of the deceased husband. He could redeem the family, and purchase back the husband's land. This process is explained in Deuteronomy and Leviticus. It applied to the closest living male relative, if a direct brother no longer existed.

> If brothers dwell together, and one of them dies and has no son, the widow of the dead man shall not be married to a stranger outside the family; her husband's brother shall go in to her, take her as his wife, and perform the duty of a husband's brother to her. (Deuteronomy 25:5)

> If one of your brethren becomes poor, and has sold some of his possession, and if his redeeming relative comes to redeem it, then he may redeem what his brother sold. (Leviticus 25:25)

Boaz promised that he would resolve this with this relative that very day, which he did. The primary kinsman said he would be Naiomi's redeemer, until he realized he also had to redeem Ruth. He said that would mar his own inheritance. He told Boaz that Boaz could redeem them. [Note: Moabites were descendants of the incestuous relationship between Lot and his daughter. One of the sons was Moab. They became idolaters. The land of Moab was cursed by God (Hickey, 2009, 21). This first kinsman did not want this mar against himself. Boaz decided he would redeem them and marry Ruth. He proclaimed this to all the elders (Ruth 4:9–11).

Something was drawing Naomi back to Bethlehem – including the family land. The ancient Israelites had a totally different perspective about land and property rights than we do. For them, God owned all the land, but He distributed it amongst all the Israelite families. Each parcel of land was supposed to stay connected forever with the family who received it. The people were supposed to take good care of the land and use it to grow food for themselves and others. But they were not supposed to sell the land outside of the family. And if, because of poverty or debt, it became necessary for a family to sell their land, they always retained the right to buy it back whenever they could. They even had the right to have a rich relative buy the land back for them so it could stay connected with the family. This relative was called a kinsman-redeemer. Maybe Naomi allowed herself to think of the possibility of somehow having the family land near Bethlehem restored to her. It then became so through Boaz.

Boaz was Naomi and Ruth's kinsman redeemer. He foreshadowed Jesus, who is also called a Kinsman Redeemer. Jesus redeemed His family (all of us) from the bondage of sin and death. His blood was the ransom payment.

After Boaz married Ruth they had a son, and they named him Obed. Obed became the father of Jesse, who became the father of David. This makes Ruth the Great Grandmother of King David, the line from which the Messiah would be born.

Ruth's decision to follow Naomi to Bethlehem gave her Boaz for her husband, and was a blessing for her. She came into the house of Israel, like Rachel and Leah, who built the house of Israel. This connected Ruth forever to Bethlehem, and the Messiah to come. This lineage of Jesus, as detailed in the first chapter of the Gospel of Matthew, provides the lineage of Jesus from Abraham to Jesus. Verses 5–6 list the lineage from Ruth and Boaz to King David.

This land purchased by Boaz was then passed down to his family line. It went to Obed, then to Jesse, David's father. This land surely became the fields where the shepherd David was grazing his father's sheep. This is the connection to specific fields in Bethlehem that are tied to the lineage of David, and ultimately of Jesus. These fields have another special significance, which we will study later.

BOAZ

Boaz was the son of Rahab and Salmon of the Tribe of Judah (Matthew 1:5). He was nine generations after Abraham. In the Book of Joshua, Chapters 2 and 6, Rahab hid the two spies of Joshua in Jericho. Joshua sent these two spies into Jericho after Moses died, before he led the children of Israel across the Jordan River into the Promised Land. The first city they would come upon and overtake was Jericho. Rahab was a harlot, but she hid these two Israelites from the King of Jericho who was searching for them. Rahab told the spies that she knew their God had taken them out of Egypt, what He did for them, and had now given them this land. She said that the hearts of those in Jericho melted and knew that their God was truly the God of heaven and earth. She asked for kindness upon her household when they entered and overtook Jericho, just as she showed kindness to them. They told her what to do so her family would be spared (Joshua 2:17–20).

Rahab was to put a *scarlet cord* in her window to signify where her household was located. That way they would be spared. This was a symbol comparable to the blood of the lamb on the doorposts at the Passover. When Joshua and the Israelites took Jericho, they destroyed the city but spared Rahab and her household. "And Joshua spared Rahab the harlot, her father's household, and all that she had. So she dwells in Israel to this day, because she hid the messengers whom Joshua sent to spy out Jericho" (Joshua 6:25). In Israel, she married Salmon, the father of Boaz.

In her book, *Jesus Revealed in Every Book of the Bible*, Marilyn Hickey writes:

> Boaz is a beautiful picture of Jesus Christ, our Kinsman-Redeemer.

Jesus came in the flesh, was tempted in all ways as we are (He had to be the Son of Man), yet was without sin and paid the price with a perfect, sinless life – shedding His blood to be our sacrificial Lamb. He paid what was needed. The kinsman-redeemer is certainly a picture of Jesus. (Hickey, 2009, 22)

JESSE

Jesse, the son of Obed and grandson of Boaz and Ruth, lived in Bethlehem, as did his forefathers. His life in Bethlehem with his sons, including David, is revealed in 1 Samuel 16.

During this time, Saul was King over Israel. He disobeyed God and was rejected as King. God sent the Prophet Samuel to Jesse in Bethlehem saying "I am sending you to Jesse the Bethlehemite. For I have provided Myself a king among his sons" (1 Samuel 16:1). God told him not to look for physical appearance, as He looks at a man's heart instead. Jesse brought forth his sons to Samuel, but Samuel said that God did not choose any of them. He asked if there was another son, and Jesse told him that David was tending sheep in the field (Note: the fields of Boaz). Jesse sent for David and when Samuel met him, he knew that David was the one chosen by God. He anointed him as king and the Spirit of God came upon him. David was anointed on his family's land in Bethlehem, in the presence of the elders of the city.

Jesus being a descendant of Jesse is important. It was later prophesied that the Messiah would come from the line of Jesse.

> There shall come forth a Rod from the stem of Jesse; And a Branch shall grow out of his roots. The Spirit of the Lord shall rest upon Him. (Isaiah 11:1–2)

> And in that day there shall be a Root of Jesse, Who shall stand as a banner to the people; For the Gentiles shall seek Him. (Isaiah 11:10)

DAVID

Even though David was anointed as king, he did not immediately become king. Saul remained king, but the Spirit of God had left Saul. Saul was distressed and sought someone to soothe him with a harp. That person was David. He became an armor bearer to Saul. Later Saul hated him and hunted him down. David learned an important lesson during this time. He learned how to be submitted to authority (even authority that wanted to kill him), so he could learn to be in authority for the children of God. In time, David became king. The line from Ruth and Boaz to David was now chosen, and David would be the lineage from which the Messiah would be born.

The Lord taught David for many years before he was put on the throne. He understood submitting to authority. Even when that authority wanted to kill him, he remained submitted. In his book *A Tale of Three Kings*, Gene Edwards explains a story of brokenness, submission and authority. It is of King Saul, David and Absalom. Of the story of David when King Saul wanted to kill him, he writes:

> How does a man know when it is finally time to leave the Lord's anointed – especially the Lord's anointed after the order of King Saul?

> David never made that decision. The Lord's anointed made it for him. The king's own decree settled the matter! "Hunt him down, kill him like a dog." Only then did David leave. No, he fled. Even then, he never spoke a word or lifted his hand against Saul. (Edwards, 1992, 25)

David's reaction to his King wanting to kill him was to quietly retreat and not fight back. David's response ensured he did not become like King Saul.

> Better he kill me then I learn his ways. Better he kill me than I become as he is...I will not throw spears nor will I allow hatred to grow in my heart. I will not avenge. Not now. Not ever. (Edwards, 1992, 34–35)

God used David's understanding of being under authority to enable him to be in authority, to become the King of Israel, and to become the lineage from which the Messiah would be born.

After Saul's death and while in Hebron, David was anointed king over Judah. In time the Lord made David king over all of Israel (2 Samuel 5:1–2). The Lord made a covenant with David, speaking through the prophet Nathan.

> Now therefore, thus shall you say to My servant David, "Thus says the LORD of hosts: *I took you from the sheepfold, from following the sheep, to be ruler over My people,* over Israel. Moreover I will appoint a place for My people Israel…When your days are fulfilled and you rest with your fathers, *I will set up your seed after you, who will come from your body, and I will establish His kingdom.* He shall build a house for My name, and *I will establish the throne of His kingdom forever. I will be His Father, and He shall be My Son…And your house and your kingdom shall be established forever before you. Your throne shall be established forever."* (2 Samuel 7:8–10, 12–14, 16; author's emphasis)

This covenant with David established the house of David forever. Through this kingdom, the Lord would reign forever. It established the lineage from which Jesus would come. It would now come through a shepherd from Bethlehem, now the King of Israel.

> Behold, the days are coming, says the Lord, That I will raise to David a branch of righteousness; a King shall reign and prosper, and execute judgment and righteousness in the earth. (Jeremiah 23:5)

> The Lord hath sworn in truth unto David; he will not turn from it; of the fruit of thy body will I set upon thy throne. (Psalm 132:11)

The lineage from Judah (son of Jacob) to David is found in 1 Chronicles, Chapter 2 and follows.

These were the sons of Israel:

Reuben, Simeon, Levi, *Judah,* Issachar, Zebulun, Dan, Joseph, Benjamin, Naphtali, Gad and Asher.

The sons of Judah:

Er, Onan and Shelah. These three were born to him by a Canaanite woman, the daughter of Shua. Er, Judah's firstborn, was wicked in the Lord's sight; so the Lord put him to death. Judah's daughter-in-law Tamar bore *Perez* and Zerah to Judah. He had five sons in all.

The sons of Perez:

*Hezron*_and Hamul.

The sons born to *Hezron* were:

Jerahmeel, *Ram* and Caleb.

Ram was the father of:

Amminadab, and Amminadab the father of <u>Nahshon</u>, the leader of the people of Judah. Nahshon was the father of Salmon, *Salmon the father of Boaz, Boaz the father of Obed and Obed the father of Jesse.*

Jesse was the father of:

Eliab his firstborn; the second son was Abinadab, the third Shimea, the fourth Nethanel, the fifth Raddai, the sixth Ozem and *the seventh David.* (1 Chronicles 2:2–15)

In John 7:42, when Jesus was teaching at the Feast of Tabernacles, the Jews asked about who Jesus was. "Does not the Scripture tell us that the Christ will come from the offspring of David and from Bethlehem, the village where David lived?" (John 7:40–42 AMP). They talked about where the Christ would come from, and the answer was Bethlehem, the village of David. *The Jews knew from Scripture where Jesus would come from, but they did not grasp it when He was in front of them.*

CHAPTER 2
The Tower of Migdal Eder

WHAT WAS MIGDAL EDER?

Bethlehem was important to the Lord for another reason. It was the city where the lambs of His Temple flock were birthed and raised. They were birthed in the Tower of the Flock at Migdal Eder, and they were raised in the surrounding fields just outside of Bethlehem.

The fields of the Kinsman Redeemer Boaz were in Bethlehem. Although not stated in Scripture, it is most probable that David was actually raising his flock for sacrifices in the Tabernacle on the land of the Kinsman Redeemer. These sheep were the foreshadowing of the true Kinsman Redeemer that would be born in this land – Jesus.

Micah 4:8 is one of our foundational Scriptures, and lists the Tower of the Flock, which is Migdal Eder in Bethlehem. This is the place that provided the protection for God's Temple Flock as they were birthed. It was the location where the shepherds that cared for the Temple Flock stood guard over them. Several translations of Micah 4:8 follow to ensure the true meaning comes forth. This verse not only mentions the Tower (Watchtower) of the Flock but also explains that the kingship will return to Jerusalem (which was fulfilled in Jesus). First, let's focus on the first part of this verse.

> *And you, O tower of the flock,*
> *The stronghold of the daughter of Zion,*
> To you shall it come,

Even the former dominion shall come,
The *kingdom* of the daughter of Jerusalem. (NKJV; author's emphasis)

And thou, *O tower of the flock,* the strong hold of the daughter of Zion, unto thee shall it come, even the first dominion; the kingdom shall come to the daughter of Jerusalem. (KJV; author's emphasis)

As for you, *Tower of Eder, (or tower of the flock)*
hill of Daughter Zion,
as for you it will come,
the former dominion will come, the royal power
belonging to Daughter Zion. (Common English Bible; author's emphasis)

And you, *watchtower for the flock,*
fortified hill (flock) of Daughter Zion, the former rule will come to you, sovereignty will come to Daughter Jerusalem.
(Holman Christian Standard Bible; author's emphasis)
As for you, *tower (Migdal-eder) of the flock,* Hill of the daughter of Zion, To you it will come - Even the former dominion will come, The kingdom of the daughter of Jerusalem. (New American Standard Bible; author's emphasis)

Each translation describes the "tower of the flock" or the "watchtower of the flock" which is "Migdal Eder" in the first part of this verse. This is referring to the location at Bethlehem where there was a tower or watchtower to guard over the Temple flock. This is referred to in the Jewish Mishnah, which is a recording of the Jewish Oral Law. It was initially recorded in written form in approximately 200 A.D. The Mishnah was a way for the rabbis to teach the law to their students in a codified manner, rather than have to go through each of the books of the Torah (the books of Moses; the first five books of the Old Testament) - (jewishvirtuallibrary.org). Migdal Eder is listed in the book of Shekelim in the Mishnah, specifically Shekelim 7:4.

An animal that was found between Jerusalem and Migdal Eder, or a similar distance in any direction, the males are [considered] burnt offerings. The females are [considered] peace offerings. Rabbi Yehuda says, those which are fitting as a Pesach (peace) offering are [considered] Pesach offerings if it is thirty days before the festival. (http://www.sefaria.org/Mishnah_Shekalim.1.1; author's emphasis)

Migdal Eder, being the location of the Temple Flock, is also explained in the Commentary of Matthew Henry for Micah 4:8.

It seems to be put for Jerusalem itself, or for Zion the *tower of David*. All the sheep of Israel flocked thither three times a year; it was the *stronghold*…or castle, of the *daughter of Zion*. (http://www. biblegateway.com/resources/matthew-henry/Mic.4.8-Mic.4.13)

TOWERS

In his book, *The New Manners and Customs of the Bible*, James M. Freeman writes about towers for the protection of vineyards or use by shepherds.

The tower was designed as a place of temporary dwelling for the guard…it was his job to keep away the thieves and wild beasts. The tower was sometimes used as a temporary abode… Many towers were frail structures lasting only the one season; others were more durable, being made of stone. They were circular or square in shape, and varied in height… The towers could also be used during times of war to watch enemy movements in the distance. Similar towers were built in the country for use by shepherds. (Freeman, 455)

2 Chronicles 26:9-10 explains that King Uzziah of Judah built towers in Jerusalem and in the desert. Isaiah 5:1-2 discusses a tower built in a vineyard. Matthew 21:33 explains about a certain landowner who planted a vineyard and set a hedge around it, dug a winepress in it and built a tower. Migdal Eder (flock-tower) was a watch-tower built for the protection of the

flocks against robbers, animals or anything else that could cause a blemish. (2 Kings 18:8; 2 Chr. 26:10; 27:4)

The Location of Migdal Eder

Micah 4:8 states that the tower is the fort, stronghold, fortified hill and citadel of the daughter of Zion. Bethlehem held this position in relation to Jerusalem. It was on the main road between Jerusalem and Hebron. Coming up from the south from Hebron, Bethlehem was on a high point approach on the way to Jerusalem.

To verify this, the answer is found in a writing of a man who was a photographer and walked from Jerusalem to Bethlehem at Christmas in 2007. He said that this was an important thing for him to do. I understand that because I have a strong need to walk the lands of Bethlehem too. Since he is walking from Jerusalem to Bethlehem, think of this in reverse to Micah 4:8. He wrote:

> *From Jerusalem the path is downhill, then up.* Rarely is any land consistently flat in this mountainous region. As I ascended the last hill before Bethlehem I saw the wall that encircles the city. Behind the wall—and here it is truly a wall, 8 m high, solid concrete about 8 cm thick, with watchtowers—stand the settlements, 8 of them at least—Har Homa, Gilo, Har Gilo, *Ephrata*, Neve Daniyel, Teqoa, Rosh Zurim, and Elazar—which also surround the holy city. (Schiel, Skip. *Walk Jerusalem to Bethlehem.* Teeksa Photography. 2007. https://skipschiel.wordpress.com/2007/12/25/walk-jerusalem-to-bethlehem; author's emphasis)

The topography of the land shows that Bethlehem is on a hill. Bethlehem is actually slightly higher in elevation than Jerusalem. Also note in the quote from Skip Shiel that "Ephrata" is a settlement of Bethlehem. Micah 5:2 lists both Bethlehem and Ephrata together as if one.

We may not all have the opportunity to walk the lands of Bethlehem in person. If you can, I encourage you to use Google Earth to visualize the terrain of Bethlehem, especially in 3D view. It will prove to you the things that are being explained here with regard to the land's topography. In understanding my book, the terrain is most important. When exploring Scripture, understanding the land is important since it is part of the context of the narrative. A good explanation of this can be found in the book, *Fifth Gospel* by Bargil Pixner. As stated in the Preface of the *Fifth Gospel* "...the places in which God revealed himself to man still remain ever present. So the soil of the Holy Land as the scene of the events centering around the Person of Jesus can be understood as a Fifth Gospel..." (1992, 7). What the author is saying is that the geography of the Holy Land is extremely important to understanding the whole revelation of the Gospels. It can be seem as if it were almost another Gospel, especially because we can go to those places today. We can let the land speak to us as if we had been there when the events occurred. That is why knowing the location of the birthplace of Jesus and the Tower of the Flock are so important.

Returning to the Old Testament, Genesis 35:9–20 describes the travels of Jacob and Rachel. Jacob and Rachel were moving south from Bethel towards Bethlehem (having passed through Jerusalem, although that is not noted in Scripture). Bethel was ten miles north of Jerusalem, and Bethlehem was about five miles south of Jerusalem. Rachel died before reaching Bethlehem (which means they were to the north of Bethlehem), and was buried along the road there. Scripture then says that Jacob went beyond Migdal Eder, but probably did not travel far, especially with a newborn baby and loss of his wife.

At the website "Searching the Scriptures.net," there is a link that shows the travels of Jacob on this journey. Bethel, Rachel's tomb, and Bethlehem are shown on a map. It can be found at: http://www.searchingthescriptures. net/main_pages/free_bible_land_maps/map022.htm, if you want to study this further.

We know from Scripture that Migdal Eder is located at Bethlehem. Bethlehem was also referred to as Ephrata. So where was Migdal Eder located? Where is it in relation to Bethlehem, Rachel's tomb, and to the Church of the Nativity, where tradition says Jesus was born?

In studying this area today, there are a few known locations. Rachel's tomb is a visited Holy Site, even to this day. We also know of the Church of the Nativity, which is the probable location of Jesus' birth. Now we just need to find the location of Migdal Eder. It is important because it is the location of the Tower for the Temple flock and the shepherds were most likely in the surrounding area when the angels appeared to them.

The person who best understood the "Tower of the Flock" was Alfred Edersheim. According to the Alfred Edersheim author page on the Christian Classics Ethereal Library, he lived from 1825–1889. He was born in Vienna, Austria to Jewish parents. He became a scholar of the Jewish faith and the Life of Christ. In 1845, he moved to Hungary, became a Christian, and entered the Christian ministry. In 1875, he became an Episcopalian and was ordained as a priest in the Church of England. He taught at Oxford University and wrote several books. (ccel.org)

Note: The Christian Classics Ethereal Library is an organization dedicated to making Christian Classic literature widely available. It is highly recommended to use this website in research.

Alfred Edersheim had probably the best research and is the most often quoted on Migdal Eder. An excerpt of his writing from *The Life and Times of Jesus the Messiah* on this subject follows:

> And yet Jewish tradition may here prove both illustrative and helpful. That the Messiah was to be born in Bethlehem was a settled conviction. Equally so, was the belief, that He was to be revealed from Migdal Eder, "the tower of the flock." (1883, 208)

What he is saying here was that the Messiah Jesus was to be revealed from Migdal Eder. This means that Jesus was born at Migdal Eder. This is the most important fact in this study. Jesus was born at the Tower of the Flock!

Let's examine Micah 4:8 once again, focusing on the second part. It says that the Messiah would be revealed from here.

And you, O tower of the flock,
The stronghold of the daughter of Zion,
To you shall it come,
Even the former dominion shall come,
The kingdom of the daughter of Jerusalem. (NKJV; author's emphasis)

This verse states that *to* the Tower of the Flock (Migdal Eder), *the former dominion* (the Lord God) *shall come* or be revealed, bringing His kingdom.

Coupled with Micah 5:2, which is a prophecy that the Messiah will be born in Bethlehem, a connection is made between the Tower (Watchtower) of Migdal Eder, Bethlehem and the birth of Jesus here. *This prophetically means that Jesus would be born there – and revealed there. He was revealed to the shepherds of the Temple flock. This meant that these were not regular shepherds either.*

Dr. Charles Dyer, host of the program "The Land and the Book" on Moody Bible Radio, explains in his teaching is called "Shepherds: More than Field Hands," and may be accessed through The Land and the Book website. He references some of the studies from Alfred Edersheim's that were already mentioned. He then states:

> About a thousand years after Rachel's death, the prophet Micah spoke about the still-future birth of Israel's Messiah. Everyone knows the prediction that the Messiah was to be born in Bethlehem (Mic. 5:2), but few look at the larger context. Micah also predicted the reappearance of God's kingdom at Migdal Eder – the tower of the flock [Micah 4:8]. (www.thelandandthebook.org)

Returning to Alfred Edersheim's writings, he states:

> This Migdal Eder was not the watchtower for the ordinary flocks, which pastured on the barren sheepground beyond Bethlehem, but lay close to the town, on the road to Jerusalem. A passage in the Mishnah leads to the conclusion, that the flocks, which pastured there, were destined for Temple-sacrifices, and, accordingly, that the shepherds, who watched over them, were not ordinary

shepherds. The latter were under the ban of Rabbinism, on account of their necessary isolation from religious ordinances, and their manner of life, which rendered strict legal observance unlikely, if not absolutely impossible. The same Mishnaic passage also leads us to infer, that these flocks lay out all the year round, since they are spoken of as in the fields thirty days before the Passover - that is, in the month of February, when in Palestine the average rainfall is nearly greatest. Thus, Jewish tradition in some dim manner apprehended the first revelation of the Messiah from that Migdal Eder, where shepherds watched the Temple-flocks all the year round. Of the deep symbolic significance of such a coincidence, it is needless to speak. (1883, 209)

Here Dr. Edersheim explains that the Watchtower of the Flock was not an ordinary place, and these shepherds were not ordinary shepherds. This was the location for raising the flocks for the Temple sacrifices. The shepherds were specially trained for this most holy task.

The top of the tower, or watchtower, was the location where the shepherds took turns watching the flock to see if danger was approaching. In the tower's lower level was the area where the lambs of the Temple Flock were birthed. Both were part of the same tower. The lambs then grazed in the fields around the tower in the area of Bethlehem.

Dr. Edersheim's research and understanding of this is profound. Almost all other studies of Migdal Eder refer to his research. Let us look at some of these other writings on Migdal Eder, and the shepherds of the Temple flock. Messianic Jewish sources provide great insight.

Rabbi Mike L. Short writes of Migdal Eder. This is an excerpt of a teaching given by him at Beth El Messianic Congregation in Glendale, AZ. It was posted on the website Mayim Hayim Ministries, which has a mission statement "To educate and equip both the Jew and non-Jew for the study of their rich Hebraic heritage."

Rabbi Short explains:

> According to Edersheim in *The Life and Times of Jesus the Messiah,* in Book 2, Chapter 6, this Migdal Eder was not "the watchtower for the ordinary flocks that pastured on the barren sheep ground beyond Bethlehem, but it lay close to the town, on the road to Jerusalem. A passage from the Mishnah leads to the conclusion that "the flocks, which pastured there were destined for Temple sacrifices." (http://www.mayimhayim.org)

Notice that Rabbi Short quoted Alfred Edersheim. In this teaching, Rabbi Short also states that Migdal Eder is where Jacob pitched his tent after Rachel's death, and is the location of the "Watchtower of the Flock," where the Temple flock were birthed and protected.

Next, we will study the teaching of Kol Simcha, a Passover teaching on April 9, 2009 in Gainsville, Florida. Kehilat Kol Simcha is a Messianic Jewish Congregation. These excerpts are taken from their website. Their website says that they are a "Family-centered, English speaking Messianic Jewish Congregation in Gainesville, Florida." The Rabbi wrote this message, but his name was not identified. Once again, note his reference to Alfred Edersheim. The title of this teaching is "The Basis of Our Daily Victory – The Lamb of Migdal Eder."

His writing begins by explaining that Migdal Eder is commonly known in the Tanakh (Jewish Old Testament, written in Hebrew and Aramaic) and will lead to a most important Messianic revelation in Scripture.

There are several Hebrew words in this next citation, which will be explained here first. The Torah includes the first five Books of Moses. Bereshit is the Book of Genesis. Targums was the Aramaic translation of the Hebrew Bible. Targum Yonatan (Jonathan) is a version of the Aramaic translation, with a commentary. The Mishnah, which has been explained prior, is the way the law was written to explain to students of Scripture. He also cites Alfred Edersheim.

According to Edersheim, this Migdal Eder was not the watch

tower for the ordinary flocks which pastured on the barren sheep ground beyond Bethlehem, but lay close to the town, on the road to Jerusalem...

Not only does the Mishnah cite the importance of Migdal Eder, but...also mentioned by the Targums. Thus, Targum Yonatan, cited by Rabbi Munk, paraphrases Bereshit (Genesis) 35:23 and Micah 4:8,

> *He spread his tent beyond Migdal Eder, the place where king Messiah will reveal Himself at the end of days.* (http://www. kolsimcha.org/messages/2009/040909M.pdf)

It is most important for Christians to study the teachings of Messianic Jews and Rabbis in relation to the Hebrew understanding of the Bible. We Christians often miss so much Biblical understanding, because we are not versed in these teachings. When Scripture is studied in its original context, it is best understood. My husband, John, and learned this so well when we were in Turkey with Dr. Rick Renner studying the Churches of the Book of Revelation. When we walked the ground, saw what those early Christians saw and understood their customs, Scripture became better understood. Dr. Renner teaches from the original Greek, so the true meaning of the New Testament words is better understood. Studying Scripture from both the Hebrew and Greek enriches your enlightenment of the true Scripture meanings. If you ever get the opportunity to go to the Holy Land and walk the land, the meanings are all so enriched since the geography of the land explains so much.

CHAPTER 3
The Shepherds of the Temple Flock

WHO WERE THE SHEPHERDS?

Dr. Charles Dyer, host of the program "The Land and the Book" on Moody Bible Radio, explains the answer to this question in his teaching called "Shepherds: More than Field Hands." He references some of the studies from Alfred Edersheim that were already mentioned. He then states:

> Edersheim argues that the flocks kept at Migdal Eder were destined for temple sacrifice. The shepherds keeping watch over these sheep knew the purpose for the lambs under their care. And their job was to keep the animals under them from becoming injured or blemished. It was to those watching over animals destined for temple sacrifice that the angels announced Jesus' birth. "For today in the city of David there has been born for you a Savior, who is Christ the Lord." (Luke 2:11)
>
> The arrival of the ultimate Lamb of God was revealed to those responsible for watching over the sacrificial lambs that had always pointed toward Him. (www.thelandandthebook.org)

You see, these shepherds were the only people in the world who could recognize when the true Lamb of God arrived, based upon their care of the Temple flock.

It is likely that the shepherds in the fields of Bethlehem, to whom the angels appeared, were raising lambs in the very fields that King David once did. These were the fields that were once owned by Boaz, since they were handed down in the family. They were in the fields near the Watchtower of the Flock.

Rabbi Short also explains:

> First, we know that Migdal Eder was the watchtower that guarded the Temple flocks those who were being raised to serve as sacrificial animals in the Temple. These were not just any flock and herd. The shepherds who kept them were men who were specifically trained for this royal task. They were educated in what an animal that was to be sacrificed had to be and it was their job to make sure that none of the animals were hurt, damaged, or blemished...(http://www.mayimhayim.org/Rabbi%20Mike/Migdal%20Eder.htm).

These shepherds were not ordinary shepherds, but ones who knew how to ensure that the new lambs were without spot and blemish. This is very important.

The teaching from the Messianic Jewish Congregation, Kehilat Kol Simcha, also discusses the shepherds.

> The Special Lamb of Midgal Eder
>
> These details shed amazing light on the account of the birthplace of Yeshua [Jesus] the Messiah in the B'rit Chadasha [New Testament]. We know that He was born in Bethlehem, the region of the Migdal Eder! We also know that, like the other lambs, He was also destined to die an atoning death in Jerusalem. We know that He is the Messiah! Moreover, who was it that came to see the incarnation of the Messiah? Shepherds! Why? Because they were the royal shepherds whom, Edersheim says were designated to take care of the sacrificial flocks. Perhaps they also knew the tradition that Messiah was to appear in the latter days at Migdal Eder. (http://www.kolsimcha.org/messages/2009/040909M.pdf)

The angel's revelation was to the shepherds – the shepherds of the Temple flock. They understood what the angel's revelation meant because they would have been familiar with Scripture, especially Scripture that related to the land in which they lived and the tasks they performed.

CARE OF THE TEMPLE FLOCK

The Mishnah confirms that blemish-free sacrificial animals for the Temple were grazed at Migdal Eder. Next to the Scriptures, the Mishnah is the basic textbook of Jewish life and thought, and is traditionally considered to be an integral part of the Torah revealed to Moses on Mount Sinai. As stated in the Mishnah:

> 951 Shek. vii. 4. leads to the conclusion, that the flocks, which pastured there, were destined for Temple-sacrifices. In fact the Mishnah (Baba K. vii. 7) expressly forbids the keeping of flocks throughout the land of Israel, except in the wilderness - and the only flocks otherwise kept, would be those for the Temple-services. (Baba K. 80 a)

The angels gave the shepherds specific keys in finding the Messiah. "And this shall be a sign unto you; Ye shall find the babe wrapped in swaddling clothes, lying in a manger" (Luke 2:12 KJV). The two keys are "swaddling clothes" and that they would find the Messiah in a "manger." How would they know where to find Him from this information? Because this is exactly how they cared for the Temple flock as they were born. They knew exactly where to go – to Migdal Eder.

The Annotated Dakes Reference Bible discusses the word "swaddling." It states that:

> These were bandages tightly wrapped around the new-born child. The rank of the child was indicated by the splendor and costliness of these bands. Fine shawls and scarves were used by the rich and common cloth by the poor. Babies so wrapped looked like mummies with no sign of arms or legs. Even the head was wrapped, the eyes only being visible (1991, 58).

Here we see the term "swaddling" (swaddled here) used in Scripture, in the Book of Ezekiel.

> Again the word of the Lord came unto me, saying, Son of man, cause Jerusalem to know her abominations, And say, Thus saith the Lord God unto Jerusalem; Thy birth and thy nativity is of the land of Canaan; thy father was an Amorite, and thy mother an Hittite. And as for thy nativity, in the day thou wast born thy navel was not cut, neither wast thou washed in water to supple thee; thou wast not salted at all, nor swaddled at all. (Ezekiel 16:1-4 KJV)

Bethlehem was special because the shepherds in the fields of Bethlehem raised lambs for the Jewish temple in Jerusalem. During lambing season the sheep were brought there from the fields, as the lower level of the watchtower, which functioned as the birthing room for sacrificial lambs. Priestly shepherds "would wrap the newborn lambs in swaddling clothes" and place them in a manger "until they calmed down" to keep them "without defect", suitable to be sacrificial lambs for the sin of the Israelites.

Cooper P. Abrams III explains the significance of the "manger" in his writing, "Where was the Birth Place of the Lord Jesus?" Cooper Abrams III is a minister and maintains the website "Bible Truth." He is an Independent Fundamental Baptist missionary and pastor Calvary Baptist Church, Tremonton, Utah. He has a PhD in Theology and has many writings on the Biblical perspective. Dr. Abrams wrote this article, expounding upon the findings of Alfred Edersheim, explaining some of the things he wrote about Migdal Eder, and of his own research of this subject.

> The popular conception that the word "manger" refers to a trough where animals were fed may not be accurate. However, it could mean simply a stall. The Greek word which is translated in our English Bibles "manger" is *Yatnh phat-ne* (pronounced fat'-nay). The definition of the word is of a "stall" where animals are kept and in Luke 13:15 is translated as such. In the Septuagint (Greek translation of the Old Testament) the word means a stall or a crib (see Proverbs 14:4). The question is what kind of "stall" or manger

is the New Testament referring to, and what kind of animal was fed or housed there…

> The angels only told the shepherds that they would find the Babe wrapped in *"swaddling cloths and lying in a manger."* There was no need for the angels to give these shepherds directions to the birth place because they already knew. These were the men who raised sacrificial lambs that were sacrificed in the Temple. When the angelic announcement came, they knew exactly where to go, as Luke 2 indicates, for the sign of a manger could only mean *their* manger at the tower of the flock! *You cannot explain the meaning or direction of the sign they were given or their response unless you have the right manger and the right shepherds!* (bibletruth.org; author's emphasis)

As stated before, these clues of finding a babe in swaddling clothes, lying in a manger, pointed them directly to Migdal Eder. Luke 2 says that they went with haste. They knew exactly where to go. These shepherds had to certify the new born lambs as being without spot or blemish. These shepherds were the only people on earth who could certify the birth of the true Passover Lamb. And they did.

The following is from a teaching "The Birth – Revisited" by haRold Smith on his website, http://hethathasanear.com/Birth.html. I also encourage you to read the entire article. haRold Smith says that the original readers of Luke's Gospel would have understood the religious significance of the shepherds watching their flocks by night, as them being the lambs of the Temple flock.

> During lambing season the sheep were brought to the tower from the fields, as the lower level functioned as the birthing room for sacrificial lambs. Being themselves under special rabbinical care, these priests would strictly maintain a ceremonially clean birthing place. Once birthed, the priestly shepherds would routinely place the lambs in the hewn depression of a limestone rock known as "the manger" and "wrap the newborn lambs in swaddling clothes,"

preventing them from thrashing about and harming themselves "until they had calmed down" so they could be inspected for the quality of being "without spot or blemish"...

Every event in Yeshua's (Jesus') life pointed toward His prophesied death. On the night of His birth, an angel appeared to the shepherds who were out in the fields, "keeping watch over their flock by night" and instructed them: "you will find a baby wrapped in swaddling cloths, lying in the manger" (Luke 2). The shepherds immediately responded, "Let us now go to Bethlehem and see this thing that has come to pass, which YHVH has made known to us" (v. 15). Where would they have known to go - since there were no directions provided?

He continues to explain that in the original Greek, the words are not "in a manger", but "in *the manger.*" They knew exactly where to go – to "*the manger*" just as they were told. There they would also understand that the Babe was in "swaddling cloths" just like they would do. As it says in the New American Standard translation – "and the baby as He lay in the manger." Notice that it lists "*the manger.*"

The sign of "*the manger*" could only mean "*the manger*" at the base of the Tower of the Flock. You cannot explain the meaning or direction of the sign they were given or their response unless you have the right manger, the right shepherds and the proper Hebraic perspective...

He summarizes by saying that its is like those early Christians reading Luke would understand that the The Lamb of God would come from Bethlehem – just as all the lambs for sacrifice came from there. They would have been able to understand the imagery. Also remember that many early Christians were Jews and would be completely familiar with where the lambs for the Temple sacrifices were kept.

The declaration to the shepherds was a prophetic sign to Israel. The shepherds were given the announcement by the angels of the Lord, and Scripture says that made know the event. But there is no record that the people who heard even responded. There is no record that anyone in the area came to see the Messiah. Even at His birth, the Jews missed the time of His visitation.

To close, let us end where we started with Bethlehem.

> So Rachel died and was buried on the way to *Ephrath (that is, Bethlehem)*. And Jacob set a pillar on her grave, which is the pillar of Rachel's grave to this day. Then Israel journeyed and pitched his tent beyond *the tower of Eder*. (Genesis 35:19–21 NKJV; author's emphasis)

Why did Jacob go to Migdal Eder? It existed at that time. He continued on the Hebron road, heading south. Migdal Eder was just to the east of the Hebron Road. This is not stated in Scripture, but makes perfect sense. He went there because there were shepherds there, and they knew how to care for baby lambs. He had a new baby and went to them to help him care for his newborn, Benjamin. Benjamin was taken to Migdal Eder after he was born, and later Jesus was born there.

What is the significance of both Benjamin and Jesus being at the same location as babes? Important people that had a distinct connection to Jesus came from the line of Benjamin. Saul was the first king of Israel (1 Samuel 9–10), and Jesus is the last King. The Apostle Paul, called by Jesus, was also of the tribe of Benjamin.

CHAPTER 4
The Birth Of Jesus

LUKE CHAPTER 2

1 And it came to pass in those days that a decree went out from Caesar Augustus that all the world should be registered. 2 This census first took place while Quirinius was governing Syria. 3 So all went to be registered, everyone to his own city.

4 Joseph also went up from Galilee, out of the city of Nazareth, into Judea, to the city of David, which is called Bethlehem, because he was of the house and lineage of David, 5 to be registered with Mary, his betrothed wife, who was with child. 6 So it was, that *while they were there, the days were completed for her to be delivered.* 7 And she brought forth her firstborn Son, and *wrapped Him in swaddling cloths, and laid Him in a manger,* because *there was no room for them in the inn.*

8 Now there were in the same country shepherds living out in the fields, keeping watch over their flock by night. 9 And behold, an angel of the Lord stood before them, and the glory of the Lord shone around them, and they were greatly afraid. 10 Then the angel said to them, "Do not be afraid, for behold, I bring you good tidings of great joy which will be to all people. 11 For there is born to you this day in the city of David a Savior, who is Christ the Lord. 12 *And this will be the sign to you: You will find a Babe wrapped in swaddling cloths, lying in a manger.*" 13 And suddenly there was with the angel a multitude of the heavenly host praising

God and saying: **14** "Glory to God in the highest, And on earth peace, goodwill toward men!"

15 So it was, when the angels had gone away from them into heaven that the shepherds said to one another, "Let us now go to Bethlehem and see this thing that has come to pass, which the Lord has made known to us." **16** And *they came with haste and found Mary and Joseph, and the Babe lying in a manger.* **17** Now when they had seen Him, *they made widely known* the saying which was told them concerning this Child. **18** And all those who heard it marveled at those things which were told them by the shepherds. **19** But Mary kept all these things and pondered them in her heart. **20** Then the shepherds returned, glorifying and praising God for all the things that they had heard and seen, as it was told them (Luke 2:1-20 NKJV - author's emphasis).

As explained at the beginning of "The Lamb Eternal," my study on the birth of Jesus began a few years ago at Christmas. I asked the Lord a simple question. "Why was Jesus born in a manger?" The answer I received from the Holy Spirit was "because He had to begin His life as a Lamb." This study took us through the book *The Lamb Eternal* and now takes us to the events of the birth of Jesus, as recorded in the second chapter of Luke.

There are key points to cover in this study from this passage, and those phrases have been italicized. Mary and Joseph had been in Bethlehem before Jesus was born. Verse 6, states that "while they were there…," the time came for Mary to give birth. Verse 7 states that she delivered her firstborn Son, wrapped him in swaddling cloths, laid Him in a manager, and that there was no room for them in the inn. An understanding of each of these passages is important in this study.

WHILE THEY WERE THERE

We often read the story of the birth of Jesus as Joseph and Mary coming into Bethlehem on a donkey. When they get there, they find there is no room for them in the inn and Mary is about to give birth, so they have to go to a stable for animals. This story we have come to understand is not accurate, based upon what we have already studied. But there is more than that. God would not put to chance anything about the birth of His Son on earth for the redemption of mankind. Both Joseph and Mary were from the royal line of David, and Bethlehem was David's city. Verse 4 explains that Joseph was "of the house and lineage of David." They probably went to the family home in Bethlehem and were staying there. They were in Bethlehem for an unknown period of time before Mary gave birth.

No Room in the Inn

In his article "The Birth – Revisited" which we studied before, haRold Smith explains that tradition makes us think that Joseph and Mary had no place to go, and became "stuck" in an animal stable as a last resort to give birth to the Messiah. He says that Scripture does not support this. The Greek word for "inn" is "kataluma," which means "guest chamber" – and of the family home. Jewish family homes had a "guest chamber – kataluma" which was available for the family guests. Kataluma is translated in Luke 2:7 as "inn," however in Luke 22:11 when Jesus is seeking a place to celebrate Passover, it is translated as guest chamber. The term guest chamber is certainly a valid interpretation, and is much more in keeping with Jewish family life.

Scripture says that "while they were there" the time had come for Mary to give birth. In all likelihood they did not start on their journey when Mary was 9 months pregnant. This is almost a certainty, first of all, what husband would subject his wife to such a journey so close to the birth of their child? Second, the census ordered by the Romans most likely would have taken place during the summer so any traveling could occur during good weather. They probably had been in Bethlehem for some time when the time for Jesus to be born arrived. They had been staying in the guest chamber of the family home in Bethlehem. They were both descendants of King David, as were their families. This would have been a nice home in which they were staying.

However, when a woman gave birth, she became "ceremonially unclean." She needed to be separated from the family, so that they also would not become unclean by her blood, released during childbirth. Joseph and Mary needed to move out of the guest chamber of the family home. Their family would not have ostracized them and forced them to move to an animal stable at a time of childbirth.

Where did they go? They went to the Watchtower of the Flock. How did they know? Did the Lord tell them? Did an angel appear to Joseph in another dream? Did they understand from Scripture? Being of the linage of King David, they would know of the prophecies about the birth of the Messiah. They knew that Mary was carrying the Messiah. They understood what the Bible said about the birth of the Messiah, and how He would be revealed from Migdal Eder. The birth chamber would be ceremonially clean for the sacrificial lambs; thus clean for the birth of the Messiah. The Bible does not say explicitly, *but they went there for Jesus to be born. Then, the angels sent the shepherds of the Temple flock to certify to the world that the Messiah was born.*

The shepherds were around blood with the birth of sheep and other animals, so they could not always remain ceremonially clean. They could be around blood this time too. They also knew what to do with the Babe, one that they recognized as The Lamb of God, and certified Him to the world.

Swaddling Cloths and the Manger

Luke 2:7 states that after Jesus was born, Mary wrapped Him in swaddling cloths and laid Him in a manger. Note: The KJV and some other translations use the term "clothes" instead of "cloths."

Since the shepherds birthed the lambs of the Temple flock at the Tower of the Flock, all the provisions for the birth of The Lamb of God would have been there. What God needed next was for His Son to be "revealed." As we have studied before, that revelation came through the shepherds. The shepherds knew exactly where to go when they heard the angel say that the Babe would be wrapped in swaddling cloths and lying in a manger. They went directly to the Tower of the Flock to find Him.

Michael Norton, Pastor of Lewisville Bible Church in Lewisville, TX explains more about swaddling cloths on the website "Faith Gateway." He is quoting information presented a number of years prior by Jimmy DeYoung at a Prophecy Conference. Jimmy DeYoung is a prophecy teacher from Chattanooga, Tennessee. He discusses what he learned from Jimmy DeYoung in this Christmas message.

> DeYoung explained that the shepherds in the field had not all been the lowly shepherds that we had always assumed. They were actually priests from the Temple who were doing shepherding work to assist in the birthing of the sacrificial lambs so that they would be unblemished for sacrifice. While the shepherds were keeping watch over the flock from the top floor of the tower, the shepherd-priests would bring the pregnant sheep in from the field to the tower's bottom floor, where the sheep would give birth. As soon as a lamb was born, the priests would wrap it with strips of cloths made from old priestly undergarments. This was done to keep the lamb from getting blemished. The priests would then place the lamb onto a manger to make sure it would not get trampled. *Wow!* So when these shepherd-priests went into Bethlehem and saw the baby Jesus wrapped in cloths, lying in a manger, they must have exclaimed, "There is the Lamb of God, prepared for sacrifice, unblemished!" *They had to be excited beyond description, because they were the only ones who could have understood the sign. It was just for them from God. It was personal!*
>
> I presume that Jesus' swaddling cloths were from the same source as the lambs' cloths. Mary's cousin, Elizabeth, was married to the priest Zacharias. Elizabeth could have given her the cloths made from the priestly undergarments. It is highly probable that the first clothes that Jesus wore were the clothes of a priest. (http://www. faithgateway.com/lamb-yahweh/#.WXaHJ4jyuT8)

This is so amazing – that only God could have prepared the birth of Jesus with this exact precision. Every detail was met - even down to Jesus being wrapped in priestly garments when He was born and laid in the exact location of the lambs being born who foreshadowed Him. Whether Mary brought the cloths or they used the cloths that were already in place for the flock, Jesus was wrapped in cloth strips specifically meant for this purpose. Then God sent the shepherds of the Temple Flock to certify that the Messiah was born.

Although I came to this conclusion on my own with the guidance of our Lord by revelation, others have come to the same conclusion. Bill Blankschaen of "Faithwalkers" explains it this way on his website dated December 19, 2012. The title of his writing is "Was Jesus born away in a manger?" He summarizes what I concluded very nicely.

> Here's the theory in summary. There was place just outside of Bethlehem city, but still within the region commonly known as Bethlehem, where Passover lambs were kept by specially trained and purified shepherds. The lambs were born in this "tower of the flock" known as Migdal Eder under the watchful eye of the shepherds who would then inspect and either certify them for use as sacrifices in the temple or designate them to be released for common use. The new lambs would, according to some sources, even be wrapped in special swaddling clothes once certified…
>
> Here's what I find fascinating about the theory. First, it places Jesus' birth in the traditional location for Passover lambs to be born. Fitting, since He became the Passover Lamb of God who took away the sins of the world. Second, it explains how the shepherds knew where to go to find the newborn babe — and why it being wrapped in swaddling clothes would be significant clue. Finally, it explains why those shepherds were notified as it was their holy calling to certify Passover lambs upon birth. (http://www.patheos.com/blogs/faithwalkers/2012/12/was-jesus-born-away-in-a-manger-at-migdal-eder/accessed 3-8-17)

haRold Smith, in his teaching, "The Birth – Revisited," explains that once the lambs were born, they were placed in "the manger" which was a hewn depression in limestone rock at this location. There, according to Baba K.

vii. 7 in the Mishnah, there they would be inspected for being without spot or blemish.

The "manger" was a special place known to the shepherds. When the angels told them to go to Bethlehem and find the Babe wrapped in swaddling cloths and lying in a manger, the angels were telling them to go do their mission. haRold Smith says that the translation for the word "a" is actually "the" in the Greek. This means that the angels told them to go the "the manger." The Babe was awaiting them, being swaddled to keep free from any spot or blemish. He was ready for them to certify Him as such in the place of certification – "the manger." There was no question in their minds where to go or what they were being requested by God to do. They were the only people on earth who could complete this task. They were the shepherds of the sacrificial lambs – and of THE Lamb of God. This was their marching order from God – and they did it.

In his message "This Shall Be a Sign" by Pastor Jacob Duran "in his Letters to the Flock" of December 28, 2007, he explains the following.

> The shepherds who kept these sheep were devout men who were trained for this special task, educated in the law concerning sacrifices and the importance of protecting the lambs from anything that might blemish or make them unfit for temple sacrifice. They also knew what the ritual sacrifice of these lambs foreshadowed and looked for the promised Messiah who was able to make peace between God and fallen man.

> The announcement to the shepherds, in Luke 2:8-20, was a purposeful part of God's ultimate plan to redeem fallen man through the perfect, unblemished sacrifice of one whom John referred to as "the Lamb of God, which taketh away the sin of the world."

> When the angel sent these shepherds to Bethlehem, he was pointing the way to the very last sacrificial lamb who, once offered, would end all need for further temple sacrifice. The Lamb was the culmination of all other sacrifices that had ever been, according

to the law of Moses—the One to whom all other sacrifices had pointed—who would at last remove the enmity of our sin and make us acceptable before God.

In essence, once they had found the Lamb of God, lying in a manger, they were—for all intents and purposes—out of a job, as far as God was concerned. (http://letterstotheflock.blogspot.com/2007/12/this-shall-be-sign.html)

THE TIME OF YEAR JESUS WAS BORN

Since the Temple Flock were in the fields all year round, as we have previously studied, Jesus could have been born at any time of year. We know that Jesus was not born on December 25th. That was actually a day celebrating a pagan god before Jesus was born.

In an article entitled "Why December 25?" on the *Christianity Today* website, author Elesha Coffman explains the origin of December 25th as the birthday of Jesus. She says that for the first three centuries of the Christian church, Christmas was not even on the calendar. The early church founder, Origin (185–254 A.D.) taught that celebrating the birthdays were for pagan gods, and not our Lord. Other early church fathers, such as Clement of Alexandria (150–215 A.D.), Hippolytus (170–236 A.D.) and Polycarp (60–155 A.D.) did not feel the same, and favored different dates.

> The eventual choice of December 25, made perhaps as early as 273, reflects a convergence of Origen's concern about pagan gods and the church's identification of God's Son with the celestial sun. December 25 already hosted two other related festivals: natalis solis invicti (the Roman "birth of the unconquered sun"), and the birthday of Mithras, the Iranian "Sun of Righteousness" whose worship was popular with Roman soldiers. The winter solstice, another celebration of the sun, fell just a few days earlier. Seeing that pagans were already exalting deities with some parallels to the true deity, church leaders decided to commandeer the date and introduce a new festival... Christians first celebrated Christmas on December 25 in 336, after Emperor Constantine had declared

Christianity the empire's favored religion. (christianitytoday.com, 2008, accessed March 18, 2017)

This explains more on how December 25th was chosen as the birthday of our Lord. Since this is not Jesus' true birthdate, there is more credence that the Father would have chosen a very special date. As with the Passover signifying Jesus' death, we have seen that with the birth of Jesus nothing has been by chance. It was "God-planned." Could Jesus have been born on a Feast Day of the Lord? I propose He was.

We studied the Feast Days of the Lord from *The Lamb Eternal* book, which is the first of this two-book series. Let me provide an overview of the Feasts in case you are reading this book first, and to put the following information into a more current context. The full information can be found in Chapter 4 of *The Lamb Eternal*.

The Lord instituted the Feast Days of the Lord, and all seven are listed in order in the 23rd Chapter of Leviticus. They represent "appointed times" God called the Jews to partake with Him. These were not Jewish Feast Days, but Feast Days of the Lord. All men, even we Christians, have been extended an opportunity to meet with God and share in His blessings of these Feasts.

There are Spring and Fall Feast Days. The Spring Feast Days are the Feasts of Passover, Unleavened Bread, First Fruits and Weeks. They represent Jesus when He was here on earth as our Savior, and the coming of the Holy Spirit. The Fall Feast Days are the Feasts of Trumpets, Atonement and Tabernacles. They represent Jesus in the days to come, up to and when Jesus returns as the King of Kings.

These were given to the Jews to point the way towards the Messiah, Jesus The Lamb. The fulfillment of the Spring Feasts was in Jesus. The fulfillment of the Fall Feasts will come with the return of the Messiah.

The Spring Feasts are:

> Passover —Jesus's death as the Passover Lamb
>
> Feast of Unleaven Bread – Jesus in the grave; His body did not decay (Acts 2:27)
>
> The Feast of Firstfruits —Jesus' Resurrection; He presents His blood to the Father
>
> The Feast of Weeks —Pentecost (the outpouring of the Holy Spirit; the birthday of the Church)

It is important to note that all of the Spring Feasts actually occurred on the days that the Jews were celebrating them in the time of Christ. Jesus was living them out before their eyes. However, they missed the true meaning of each of them, just as they missed Jesus as the Messiah.

The Jews celebrate the Fall Feasts, but unless they are Messianic Jews, they do not see their true significance in Jesus for future events. We are currently living in the actual time period between the Spring and Fall feasts. These Fall Feasts occur within a short period in the Hebrew month of Tishri (September/October). What they represent to Christians is:

> Trumpets — The Rapture of the Church and the judgment of the wicked
>
> Day of Atonement — Salvation of Israel and of Gentiles still living during the Tribulation (who were not in the Rapture of the Church)
>
> Tabernacles — Establishment of the Messianic Kingdom

However in *The Lamb Eternal*, I explained that even though the Feast of Atonement is a Fall Feast, Jesus fulfilled it at his death on Calvary.

According to Perry Stone, this is the only Feast Day with *two applications*. He explained this in his teaching *New Evidence of a Pre-Tribulation Rapture* on his program *Manna Fest* on 4-22-16. Jesus fulfilled it in His death, but it also applies to the future fulfillment of the Fall Feast Days. He has more information on this in his book *Prophecies Concealed Now Revealed* for your further study.

If the Feast Day of Atonement has two applications being fulfilled by Jesus, then could it also apply to another Fall Feast Day? I propose that this is the case. Let me explain. First, turn to the book *The Feasts of the Lord* by Kevin Howard and Marvin Rosenthal.

The seventh Feast is the Feast of Tabernacles (or Sukkot). It is joyful, festive and mentioned more times in Scripture than any other Feast. It is translated "booths" in English. During this Feast Day, the Jews dwelt in temporary dwellings as a reminder of God's provision in the wilderness. The Feast of Tabernacles lasts for seven days.

> Tabernacles falls in the autumn of the year. On the Hebrew calendar it occurs on the 15th day of Tishri, the seventh month (usually late September to mid-October), only five days after the solemn Day of Atonement. (1997,136)

The Feast of Tabernacles required a pilgrimage to Jerusalem. It was considered the most important of the Feast Days. It was during this Feast that Solomon built the Temple so God could dwell with His people there. The Feast of Tabernacles speaks of man dwelling with God – and God dwelling with man. Its future fulfillment will be when Jesus returns to set up His Messianic Kingdom.

Now let's turn to the time of Lord when He was on earth to refine this thought. In the first chapter of Matthew, the angel of the Lord comes to Joseph to explain the pregnancy of Mary. This is referencing Isaiah 7:14.

> So all this was done that it might be fulfilled which was spoken by the Lord through the prophet, saying: "Behold, the virgin shall be with child, and bear a Son, and they shall call His name Immanuel, which is translated, God with us." (Matthew 1:22-23)

Jesus was called "Immanuel", or "God with us." The Feast of Tabernacles is joyfully celebrating God with us. Could Jesus have been born on the Feast of Tabernacles? Let us turn to another study to see if this is possible.

In his teaching, "The Birth Revisited" which we have studied already, haRold Smith explains that Jesus was born in the fall, during the Feast of Tabernacles. He refers to Jesus as Yeshua, the Hebrew name for Jesus. Please study his article to read this teaching in its entirety, but it will be paraphrased here. He states that Jesus was born during the Feast of Tabernacles, so I am not alone in this thinking. He calculates the length of Jesus' ministry from number of times of times Passover is listed in the Gospel of John (John 2:13, 1:33, 2:23, 5:1, 6:4 and 11:55). The final Passover is when Jesus died on Passover. This shows that Jesus' ministry lasted about 3 ½ years. If he began His ministry around age 30, then He died around age 33 ½.

He explains that through calculation, Jesus' ministry began sometime in the early fall, around the time of the Feast of Tabernacles, making His birth around that same timeframe in the fall, probably at the Feast of Tabernacles. John 1:14 states that the Word became flesh and dwelt among us. The Hebrew word for "dwell" is the same as "Tabernacle." He says that it would be just like the Father to arrange it this way (http://hethathasanear.com/Birth.html).

This is not the only way to arrive at this conclusion. Zechariah's service in the Temple is told in Luke 1:5–13; 23–24. After this time,_his wife Elizabeth became pregnant. In her 6th month, Gabriel appeared to Mary to inform her of being chosen to be the mother of Jesus (Luke 1:26–31).

So, when did Zechariah serve in the Temple? This has been calculated by several people, and following is a summary of their results. To see the complete calculations, you can go to the following sites: http://www. askelm.com/star/star006.htm; Daniel Botha's site_http://www.borntowin. net/articles/the-division-of-abijah/; and Luizius Schneider's site https:// www.luziusschneider.com /Papers/JesusDateOfBirth.htm. These three are being referenced here.

Simply put, each division ("course" in the King James) of priests was to serve for one week according to its division, except for the festivals when all priests were to serve. Zechariah was in the eighth division. Although he would serve twice in the year (spring and fall) both Schneider and askelm. com have shown that Zechariah's service in the spring is the time Luke is referring to.

Because of this we can easily determine when Zechariah was serving in the Temple. The schedule for the priests to serve started at the beginning of the Hebrew calendar in the month of Nissan, determined by the new moon of March/April. Since the first festival (Passover) was in the first month, Zechariah was actually in the Temple during the ninth week. So, this is when he received the visit from Gabriel telling him that Elizabeth would have a child.

> One would assume that Zacharias (Zechariah) would have gone home to his wife at the end of the ninth week; however, that was the week of the Feast of Weeks (see Leviticus 23:15-16), also called the Feast of Firstfruits (or Pentecost in the New Testament), when all priests were again to serve in the Temple. So Zacharias would have gone home after Pentecost, mid to late June. That is when John would have been conceived. Why is this important and what has it got to do with Jesus? Notice Luke 1:26: "Now in the sixth month . . ." (KJV)
>
> The sixth month of what? What was it talking about? It was talking about Elizabeth getting pregnant with John. It was talking about the sixth month of Elizabeth's pregnancy. (Botha, http://www.borntowin.net/articles/the-division-of-abijah/)

Based on this, we can conclude that John the Baptist was six months older that Jesus, and so we can determine when Mary visited Elizabeth (Luke 1:26, 41) and when Jesus was born.

John was conceived in late June, six months after John's conception. This would be late in December, the month Kislev, (ninth month of the Jewish calendar). This corresponds to Hanukkah – the Jewish Festival of Lights.

How appropriate if the Light of the World would have been conceived on the Festival of Lights! This is not stated in the Bible, but can be speculated based upon the timing of Biblical and Hebrew writings. Nine months from that time brings us to Tishri (7th month of the Jewish calendar) (this corresponds to September/October) which is when Sukkot (the Feast of Tabernacles) occurs, and when Jesus probably was born.

WHERE JESUS WAS BORN

To conclude this chapter, we are again turning to the article "Where was the Birth Place of the Lord Jesus?" by Cooper Abrams III. He makes some key points that are important to keep in mind in studying the birth of Jesus. Please read his full article to understand all that he is saying, but I am paraphrasing some highlights here. He makes it clear that Jesus was born at the Tower of the Flock in Bethlehem and that the shepherds were the right people to receive the announcement of the birth of the Messiah. He says that Micah uses this prophecy in Micah 4:8 to authenticate the prophecy of the birth of Christ at Migdal Edar.

Micah first discusses that the Assyrians would carry away the Northern Kingdom. Then the Babylonians would carry the Southern Kingdom into captivity. Since those events would come before the prophecy of the Messiah, he hoped that the Israelites would understand that prophecy to validate the prophecy of the Messiah, and know Him when He came to the Tower of the Flock. But it was a proof that they later ignored.

He also explains that the location where the Temple flock were born and raised was important for a short trip to Jerusalem for their eventual sacrifices. That way they could be herded along the road to Jerusalem, and their chance of being injured or disheveled from the walk was less.

The shepherds were under special Rabbinical care, so they would have maintained a ceremonially clean stable for the birthing place of the lambs, and for Jesus. The lambs birthed at the Tower of the Flock were apparently wrapped in "swaddling cloths" to protect them from injury, and were also used to wrap the Lord Jesus. Jesus was born in the very birthplace where tens of thousands of sacrificial lambs had been birthed before, foreshadowing His birth there.

When the angels told the shepherds to find the Babe, the only directions the angels gave was that they would find Him wrapped in swaddling cloths and lying in a manger. The angels gave no other directions. Why? Because, the shepherds knew exactly where to go. The sign to them of a manger meant "their manger" at the Tower of the Flock. You cannot explain the meaning or direction of the sign they were given or their response unless you have the right manger and the right shepherds!

The following is from a teaching "The Birth – Revisited" by haRold Smith.

> But, it does not take a leap of imagination to envision how Joseph and Mary, coming from a family whose local roots containing the seed of royalty went back centuries, could have found her birthing place in the sacrificial birth room of the Temple of YHVH. It would be so like the Father to arrange it this way. (http://hethathasanear.com/birth.html)

THE MAGI

We have not addressed the role of the Magi here as this part of the story of the birth of Jesus occurred two years later.

> Now when Jesus was born in Bethlehem of Judaea in the days of Herod the king, behold, there came wise men from the east to Jerusalem, Saying, Where is he that is born King of the Jews? for we have seen his star in the east, and are come to worship him. When Herod the king had heard these things, he was troubled, and all Jerusalem with him. And when he had gathered all the chief priests and scribes of the people together, he demanded of them where Christ should be born. And they said unto him, In Bethlehem of Judaea: for thus it is written by the prophet, And thou Bethlehem, in the land of Juda, art not the least among the princes of Juda: for out of thee shall come a Governor, that shall rule my people Israel. Then Herod, when he had privily called

the wise men, enquired of them diligently what time the star appeared. And he sent them to Bethlehem, and said, Go and search diligently for the young child; and when ye have found him, bring me word again, that I may come and worship him also. When they had heard the king, they departed; and, lo, the star, which they saw in the east, went before them, till it came and stood over where the young child was. When they saw the star, they rejoiced with exceeding great joy. And when they were come into the house, they saw the young child with Mary his mother, and fell down, and worshipped him: and when they had opened their treasures, they presented unto him gifts; gold, and frankincense and myrrh. And being warned of God in a dream that they should not return to Herod, they departed into their own country another way. (Matthew 2 1-12 KJV)

However, because they are intertwined in the Christmas story, we will reflect on the timing of their visit. According to Matthew, the Magi saw the sign of Jesus' birth and journeyed to pay Him homage. How would they know and why would they care? That is a source of much inquiry, however as the Magi came from Persia, it is likely due to the influence of Daniel. This would result in them knowing prophecies and looking for signs indicating the coming of the Jewish Messiah. Any further exploration is beyond the scope of this book.

For further exploration of the subject of the Magi read Matthew Henry's Commentary on Matthew 2.

CHAPTER 5
Teachings Of The Early Church

We have studied the precision of God regarding His Son, The Lamb of God. God is always precise, which leads to this simple question. How could it be that He would let His Son be born in some empty stable somewhere because there was no room available at an inn by chance? The answer is that He couldn't – and didn't. That is why Jesus was born in a precise location. The Christians of the early Church knew the location, and early Christian writers wrote about it. Imagine being a Christian in the early Church. Such a prominent place as the location of the birth of Jesus would not be lost or forgotten. It would be memorialized, and the early Christian writers explain that it was.

THE LOCATION OF JESUS' BIRTH
The location of Jesus' birth in Bethlehem goes mostly undisputed. There is too much documented evidence for it, and there is no other location thought to be a possibility. There is only one! It is at the grotto inside the Church of the Nativity. It can be established as a fact that this is the location where Jesus was born.

The Catholic Franciscan monks have a very good understanding of the history of this grotto and the church built over it. There has been very careful tracking of this location. They kept a detailed history of Bethlehem and the Church of the Nativity during their centuries of overseeing the Basilica there. Their website is named "Custodia Terrae Sanctae," or "Custody of the Holy Land." Their website is www.custodia.org and is written by the Franciscan missionaries serving the Holy Land. It has information for all the Holy Land sites that they protect and serve. For this study, follow the links for "Sanctuaries" and then "Bethlehem" to find the detailed information. Most of the following information on Bethlehem and the Church of the Nativity is summarized from their website, except where otherwise noted. Exact quotes from the "Custodia" website are specifically cited.

1ST – 4TH CENTURIES A.D.

During the 1st through the 4th centuries A.D., there were several known witnesses to the site of Jesus' birth, including Origen, Eusebius, and Jerome. They knew the location of Jesus' birth and documented it as early Church history. It is important to know what they did about this location.

Understand that Jesus' birth place was important to the early Christians and was not forgotten. It was revered. It was protected. In 70 A.D., when Jerusalem was destroyed under the Roman Emperor Titus, Bethlehem was spared. The very early Christians knew the location where Jesus was born, and protected it. During the time of the Jewish revolts under the reign of Hadrian, he built a pagan temple to the god Adonis over the Grotto of the Nativity, which was buried underneath it. This would have resulted in the destruction of the tower of Midgal Edar. However, it is felt that the grotto (cave) underneath this location was left alone in a natural state underneath. Early Christian writers, such as Eusebius, Jerome and Origen explained that there was a clear memory that this was the exact location where Jesus was born. Unfortunately, it was in the hands of pagans for centuries while they idol-worshipped above it. This was Satan trying to rub out the memory of this holy place. This explains why no sign of the tower remains, but the lower chamber, a cave, still does. But amidst all of this, Jesus' birth site was nonetheless preserved underneath.

The "Jewish Virtual Library" also has information about this location during this time. It records that after the Second Jewish Revolt, Emperor Hadrian tried to eradicate the places of worship of the Christians and Jews by placing idols at holy sites. The Second Jewish Revolt occurred in 132–135 A.D. after the Emperor Hadrian, who rose to power in 118 A.D., turned from being sympathetic to the Jews, to turning against them. In 118

A.D., the early Christians were worshipping at the site of the grotto of the Nativity. This means that within the first 100 years after the death of Jesus, this site was known and revered. Under Hadrian, the Jews and Christians lost, and many were sold into slavery and were heavily persecuted. This lasted until his death in 138 A.D., but the idolatry he started continued at the holy sites for some time (http://www.jewishvirtuallibrary.org/jsource/Judaism/revolt1.html). It is sad to say, but the pagans were the ones guarding this holy site for almost two hundred years because the Jews were not allowed to be in Bethlehem at this time in history.

One of the earliest Popes, St. Evaristus (Pope from 100–109 A.D.), was born in Antioch, but his father was a native of Bethlehem. It is probable that this also helped preserve the memory of this location. Let us look at some of these early Christian writers who documented this location.

"The first evidence of a cave in Bethlehem being venerated as Christ's birthplace is in the writings of Justin Martyr around 160 A.D." (sacred-destinations.com).

The early Christian theologian, Origen Adamantius (commonly just known as Origen), wrote about the location of Jesus' birth. Origen lived from 185-254 A.D., so his information is very early in Church history about this location (Catholic Encyclopedia http://www.newadvent.org/cathen/11306b.htm). He was able to observe the worship of the holy places in the Holy Land, including the Grotto of the Nativity. He explained that the cave where Jesus was born and the manger located there conformed to the Gospels regarding the birthplace of Jesus. In his writing *Contra Celsus*, Book 1, Chapter 51, Origen states:

> There is shown at Bethlehem the cave where He was born, and the manger in the cave where He was wrapped in swaddling-clothes. And this sight is greatly talked of in surrounding places, even among the enemies of the faith, it being said that in this cave was born that Jesus who is worshipped and reverenced by the Christians.

The Emperor Constantine proclaimed religious freedom to the Roman Empire in 313 A.D., with the Edict of Constantine. This began an era of religious freedom for Christian worship and reverence of the holy places. In 325 A.D., St. Macarius told Constantine about the poor condition of the Holy Places. With the strong influence of his mother, Helena, restoration of the site and construction for the Church of the Nativity and other Christian sites in the Holy Land was begun. "An established local tradition enabled the architects to begin work at once in 326. The local people knew that at the end of the village among the trees was the cave in which was born Jesus Christ" (www.custodia.org).

Eusebius Pamphili (commonly just known as Eusebius) was a Greek historian who lived in the era of the Emperor Constantine. He was the bishop of Caesarea and lived from about 260–341 A.D. He wrote the story of the early Church from the time of Christ to Constantine and became known as the "Father of Early Church History." He was a biographer of Constantine and wrote a great deal about the holy places and the churches Constantine built over them. He also described the architectural evolution of the cave now called the Grotto of the Nativity to the church being built over it. He explained that Helena, Constantine's mother, consecrated two shrines, one at the site of Jesus' ascension and the other where Jesus was born. Eusebius stated the following in his writing *Church History, the Life of Constantine, Oration in Praise,* Chapter XLIII – A Farther Notice of the Churches at Bethlehem*:*

> For without delay she dedicated two churches to the God whom she adored, one at the grotto which had been the scene of the Savior's birth; the other on the mount of His ascension. For He who was "God with us" had been submitted to be born in a cave of the earth, and this place of His nativity was called Bethlehem by the Hebrews.

An important writer of the 4th century regarding the location of Jesus' birth was St. Jerome. In 396 A.D., he wrote that from the time of Hadrian to Constantine, a span of about 180 years, pagan worship occurred at the Holy Places, including over the cave where Jesus was born.

In 384 A.D., St. Jerome moved into a two-room cave under the Church of the Nativity to learn Hebrew so he could translate the Old Testament from Hebrew into Latin. This became the *Latin Vulgate*, and it took him 30 years. Until the 20th Century, this was the official Bible version for Catholics.

> He carved out his own tomb in one of the cave walls and also tombs for some of the Christian Saints from that day, such as St. Paula and St. Eusebius, his successor. His body no longer exists there. It was transferred to Constantinople and then to Rome where it rests today in the Basilica of St. Mary Major (http://www.seetheholyland.net/st-jerome's-cave).

Jerome prepared his own tomb at this location, because he was *sure* that this is where our Lord was born.

This historical documentation bridges the gap between the time of Christ and the end of the fourth century. It was undisputed at that time where Jesus was born. In 339 A.D., St. Jerome wrote "but the site of the birth of Jesus remained a visible witness" (http://www.custodia.org). This was in spite of the desecration by the pagans. His devotion to these sites made of him a witness to the tradition of this place, to which he felt himself linked by his profound and intimate reflections on the incarnation of Our Lord Jesus.

5TH – 14TH CENTURIES

This large Basilica over the Church of the Nativity survived until its destruction during the Samaritan Revolt of 529 A.D. Around 360 A.D., monastic monks and nuns began to congregate in the Jerusalem and Bethlehem areas. St. Paula established a monastery for nuns and St. Jerome for the monks. St. Jerome died in 420 A.D., but the monastic life survived until 489 A.D.

In 527 A.D., Emperor Justinian became the Emperor of the Byzantine Empire. He rebuilt the Church of the Nativity after the destruction caused in the Samaritan Revolt. Eutichius of Alexandria records this fact. There was a Persian invasion in 614 A.D, but the Church was spared from destruction. The invaders saw a mosaic of the Persian wise men coming to visit Jesus. They revered their ancestors, and spared the church. This continued through the Muslim occupation. The Crusaders arrived in 1099 A.D. The church was in good shape, but they made some upgrades and also built a monastery. In 1293, the Crusaders were driven out of Bethlehem and the Muslims used the holy places for political means.

The Archeological Study Bible by Zondervan Press explains this about Jesus' birthplace site. It is within the study section for Micah 5:2.

> Very early church tradition locates Jesus' birth in a cave in Bethlehem, over which the Emperor Hadrian constructed a shrine to a Roman deity. Later, the Christian Emperor Constantine erected a church building over the cave. After its partial destruction by Samaritans in the sixth century, the Church of the Nativity was rebuilt by the Emperor Justinian and still stands today as one of the most ancient church buildings in existence. (2005,1487)

14ᵀᴴ CENTURY – PRESENT

In 1333, the Franciscans began residence in the Augustinian monastery and remain to this day. In 1347, they started officiating at the Basilica of the Nativity. In the 16th Century, a conflict arose between the Franciscans and the Greek Orthodox Church, but the Franciscans have maintained their presence there and continue to provide guardianship here. "Their history of this site remains intact and solidifies the fact that this is the location of the birth of Christ. They can trace the authenticity of this site from the time of Jesus to the present" (www.custodia.org).

A recent discovery also supports this. In the early 1960s, there was excavation in the area by Father Farina. He was able to prove that the Grotto and other subterranean passages adjoining it were occupied between 700 and 587 BC, but abandoned after the Babylonian captivity. They were occupied again at the time of Christ. He found 35 tombs, with 15 of them below ground, all prior to Constantine. "The early Christians desired to be buried near a holy place…how much more near a place sanctified by the Birth of Christ!" (www.custodia.org). He found the empty tombs of Saints Paula, Eustochium and Jerome. He says that seeing the tomb of St. Jerome supports what St. Jerome wrote.

The fact that the cave showed signs of occupancy in the centuries before Christ, is reflective of the long term use of this site. It supports the fact that it was the foundation for the Tower of the Flock – an already revered site.

THE SHEPHERDS FIELDS

The tradition regarding the location of the Shepherd's fields is complicated. There are three sites identified as possibilities - one by the Orthodox Church, one by the Catholic Church and one by the Protestants.

These locations are all downhill from the Church of the Nativity, all in the valley below the heights and all are in close proximity to the Church. Because of the size of the Temple flock necessitated by the daily sacrifices, all of these locations could have been, and probably were, areas where the Temple flocks grazed. Also because of the size of the flocks, there were certainly quite a few shepherds. The Bible doesn't specify the number of shepherds that the angels appeared to, but it probably was quite a few.

The Franciscans are not alone in this thinking that the cave where Jesus was born is at the grotto under the Church of the Nativity. In his teaching, Where was the Birth Place of our Lord Jesus?" in a section called "Is the Cave Under the Basilica of the Nativity the birth place of Jesus?" Cooper Abrams III explains that:

> A modern topographical map shows the traditional place of the Shepherd's Field as being about 300 meters from the Basilica of the Nativity on the edge of Bethlehem. The site has a long history as the place of the birth of Christ going back to Origen of Alexander in the 2nd Century.

I invite you to use Google Maps in 3D mode to look at the location of the Church of the Nativity and the Shepherds' Fields. When you see this, you will see how much sense it makes for these two locations to truly be the sites for the Tower of the Flock at the high point above the Shepherds Fields. If you ever get the opportunity to go to the Church of the Nativity and walk the Shepherds Fields, you will understand.

This is a good indication that the Church of the Nativity is the correct location for the Tower of the Flock because of its proximity and geography in relation to the Shepherds fields. Scripture proves that Jesus was born at the Tower of the Flock. The tower of the flock does not exist today, and archaeology has not found its ruins because the Romans built a temple in its place to desecrate Jesus' birthplace. Because the Church of the Nativity is from post-Scriptural times, we cannot "prove" that it is the location of the Tower of the Flock. But from the early Church times, the grotto under the Church has been memorialized as the location of the birth of Jesus. It was guarded, protected and written about from then until now. It goes undisputed that this is the location of Jesus' birth. From the geography of the area, the grotto also fits as the "cave" lower level of the Tower of the Flock, in relation to the Shepherds' Fields. We can then conclude that the site of the Church of the Nativity and the Tower are one and the same. As such, the cave (grotto) under the Church of the Nativity is the lower chamber of the Tower of the Flock. There is no doubt in my mind.

When I (Dr. Christine) was in Bethlehem and at the grotto in the Church of the Nativity, I was overcome by the presence of the Holy Spirit. There was no doubt in my mind that I was at the actual birthplace of Jesus. But now this documentation adds proof to the presence of God that I was experiencing. There is no doubt that the grotto under the Church of the Nativity is indeed the location where Jesus, the Lamb of God was born. I have all the proof I need; the Holy Spirit speaking to my spirit.

CONCLUSION

Jesus *is* The Lamb of God. He has been The Lamb since before the foundation of the world. Jesus is The Lamb of the Father, who gave His Lamb so we could be united with Him again. If people created and maintained stables (mangers) for the lambs for the Temple sacrifices, how much more would the Father have prepared a special stable (manger) for His Son, The Lamb of God to enter this world. Jesus was not born in just any stable with any manger for animals. Jesus was born in "The Manger" created for God's Plan from before the creation of the world. He prepared that special location throughout the Old Testament. He set signs in His Word and by events for this specific location. God had this plan to deliver His Son into the world in a very special place – the "Tower of the flock." *Jesus was born in "The Manger" in "The Tower of the Flock" in Bethlehem, as THE Lamb of God.*

God is precise and He would not send His Son to any old place, but He sent Him to the place He had prepared for centuries. Everything was there – the location, ceremonial cleanliness, the holiness, the swaddling clothes, and the manger. The answer to my question of God has been answered. I asked "Why was Jesus born in a manger?" God spoke to my heart "He had to begin His life as a lamb." But Jesus was not any lamb, He was THE Lamb of God slain from the foundation of the world. Jesus was born at the Watchtower of the Flock, where the Temple lambs were born. Just as the sacrifice of the Temple Flock was done on Passover and were a foreshadowing of Jesus' death as The Passover Lamb – so too the birth of the Temple Flock at the Tower of Migdal Eder was a foreshadowing of the location of the birth of Jesus, The Lamb of God. How perfect and exacting is our God! Amen.

God had a plan. John the Baptist introduced Jesus to the world as The Lamb of God. And earlier He had introduced Jesus as the Lamb to the temple shepherds watching temple lambs in the fields of Boaz and David. Jesus lived life as The Lamb, and died as the Passover Lamb. It is only true to the nature of God that Jesus was born as The Lamb of God – in the special place – the "watchtower of the flock" in Bethlehem that God provided centuries before. God introduced Jesus to the temple shepherds as The Lamb of God. They knew where to go – to the tower of the flock, the special place for the birth of the lambs for God. This makes our understanding of Christmas even more meaningful that it has ever been. Praise God!

Let us review the second chapter of Luke with the enhanced understanding following (in italics).

> And it came to pass in those days that a decree went out from Caesar Augustus that all the world should be registered. This census first took place while Quirinius was governing Syria. So all went to be registered, everyone to his own city.
>
> Joseph also went up from Galilee, out of the city of Nazareth, into Judea, to the city of David, which is called Bethlehem, because he was of the house and lineage of David, to be registered with Mary, his betrothed wife, who was with child. So it was, that *while they were there*, the days were completed for her to be delivered. And she brought forth her firstborn Son, and wrapped Him in *swaddling cloths*, and laid Him in a manger, because there was *no room* for them in the inn. (Luke 2:1-7; author's emphasis)
>
> *Mary and Joseph went to Bethlehem to register in the required census in their ancestral town. The verse says "While they were there," which means that Joseph and Mary were already in Bethlehem. So they were not searching for a room, they were staying with relatives who lived in Bethlehem, since they went to their hometown, although Scripture does not say that. They would have been staying in the family guest chamber (kataluma). There*

was "no room for them" because during and after the birth, Mary would have been considered "unclean" due to the blood associated with childbirth. She was not able to remain in the same quarters as the other family members.

They went to the tower of the flock. Mary and Joseph knew that their soon to be born Son was the Son of God. According to the first chapter of Luke, Jesus was called "the Son of the Highest," the "Holy One" and "the Son of God." Mary was told that God gave Jesus the throne of David forever and that He would reign over the house of Jacob forever. Of course Jesus had to be born in Bethlehem!!!

Mary and Joseph knew the Temple lamb birthing process. They understood that Jesus was the Lamb of God. They received direction from God, because God the Father was precise about where His Son needed to be born. It was the place prepared long in advance with the birthing of the lambs for the Temple sacrifices. All of the Temple lambs being birthed here were a foreshadowing of this very moment when THE Lamb of God would be born here. That was the first sign that the Father sent to the world (through the shepherds) that this was His Son, the Messiah.

Mary wrapped Jesus in swaddling clothes (cloths from the garments of the Temple priests) covering Jesus in the clothes of a high priest right from birth.

Now there were in the same country *shepherds living out in the fields,* keeping watch over their flock by night. And behold, an angel of the Lord stood before them, and the glory of the Lord shone around them, and they were greatly afraid. Then the angel said to them, "Do not be afraid, for behold, I bring you good tidings of great joy which will be to all people. For there *is born* to you this day in the city of David a Savior, who is Christ the Lord. And this will be *the sign* to you: You will find a Babe *wrapped in swaddling cloths, lying in a manger.*" And suddenly there was with the angel a multitude of the heavenly host praising God and saying: "Glory to God in the highest, And on earth peace, goodwill toward men!" (Luke 2:8-14; author's emphasis)

> *The shepherds who lived out in the fields all year round were the ones who raised the lambs for the year-round Temple sacrifices. The angel appeared to them, because they were the only people on earth who would be able to receive the sign from God that the Savior was born. The sign was that the Babe was wrapped in swaddling cloths and was lying in a manger. They knew precisely where to go. They went to "the manger" to find Him.*

So it was, when the angels had gone away from them into heaven that the shepherds said to one another, "Let us now go to Bethlehem and see this thing that has come to pass, *which the Lord has made known to us.*" And *they came with haste* and found Mary and Joseph, and the Babe *lying in a manger.* Now when they had seen Him, they made widely known the saying which was told them concerning this Child. And all those who heard it marveled at those things which were told them by the shepherds. But Mary kept all these things and pondered them in her heart. Then the shepherds returned, glorifying and praising God for all the things that they had heard and seen, as it was told them. (Luke 2:15–20; author's emphasis)

> *The shepherds understood that this was a message from God. They certainly knew the prophecy that the Messiah would be born in Bethlehem, as this was a prophecy about their own town. They knew where the manger was – at Migdal Eder, the tower of the flock. It was their own location. Quickly they went there. Once they saw Jesus wrapped in swaddling cloths, just like they wrapped the Temple flock, it was confirmed for them. It is how the shepherds of the flock wrapped the newborn sheep destined for the Temple sacrifices. This is because they needed to remain*

without spot or blemish. This process protected them after they were first born.

When they found Jesus, this was a confirmation for the shepherds that they found the Son of God, the true Lamb of God. Then they "made widely known" the event that had just occurred. They were "certifying" to the world that the Messiah had arrived.

It is interesting to note that Scripture does not say that others came to see Jesus. This was the first time the Jews missed the time of their visitation; but the shepherds did not.

This book looked at the birth of Jesus from the very beginning of God's plan with Abraham, Jacob and Rachael. In God's Word, the Tower of Migdal Edar and Bethlehem are introduced to us at that time. Then the for the shepherd's fields are established by the redemption of Naomi and Ruth through the kinsman-redeemer Boaz. As Ruth and Boaz are directly in the line of King David, the lands redeemed by Boaz come into the possession of the king. So, God set up the lands and made provision for there to be shepherds watching the temple flocks.

God then prepared the way with the announcement to Zacharias and the birth of John the Baptist. With the annunciation to Mary, the final fulfillment of God 's prophecies about Jesus' birth at the Tower of Migdal Edar were set in motion. The Roman census led Joseph and Mary back to Bethlehem and when the time was fulfilled for Jesus' birth, Joseph and Mary went to the tower as a ceremonially clean place for the Lamb of God to be born. As the prophecies were fulfilled the time to announce the birth came and God called on the priestly shepherds to provide witness. The angels gave the priestly shepherds all the information they needed.

"For unto you is born this day in the city of David a Saviour, which is Christ the Lord. And this shall be a sign unto you; Ye shall find the babe wrapped in swaddling clothes, lying in a manger." (Luke 2:11-12 KJV)

These shepherds provided the confirmation of the Lamb of God as the perfect Lamb born in the birthing place for the sacrificial lambs of the temple. Thus, proving that Jesus was the ultimate sacrificial lamb for all of us. His sacrifice opened the door for us all to spend eternity with God.

YOUR ETERNAL FUTURE WITH JESUS

One thing follows here that is extremely important. It addresses your eternal future. Address this question for yourself. Have you accepted Jesus as your Lord and Savior?

If the information provided in this book has convinced you that God's plan was fulfilled in Jesus and he is the Christ, the Son of the Living God and you have not accepted Him as your own personal savior, now is the time for you to do so. The process is quick and simple, the results are eternal. Do the following:

Admit that you are a sinner.
> For all have sinned, and come short of the glory of God. (Romans 3:23 KJV)

Be willing to repent of your sins.
> If we confess our sins, He is faithful and just to forgive us our sins, and to cleanse us from all unrighteousness. (1 John 1:9 KJV)

Believe Jesus died on the cross for you, and rose from the dead.
> Ye men of Israel, hear these words; Jesus of Nazareth, a man approved of God among you by miracles and wonders and signs, which God did by him in the midst of you, as ye yourselves also know: Him, being delivered by the determinate counsel and foreknowledge of God, ye have taken, and by wicked hands have crucified and slain: Whom God hath raised up, having loosed the pains of death: because it was not possible that he should be holden of it. (Acts 2:22-24 KJV)

> But now is Christ risen from the dead, and become the firstfruits of them that slept. (1Corinthians 15:20 KJV)

Invite Jesus into your heart as Lord and Savior.

> For whosoever shall call upon the name of the Lord shall be saved. (Romans 10:13 KJV)

> That if thou shalt *confess with thy mouth* the Lord Jesus, and shalt *believe in thine heart* that God hath raised him from the dead, thou shalt be saved. For with the heart man believeth unto righteousness; and with the mouth confession is made unto salvation. (Romans 10: 9,10 KJV)

Now pray this prayer to God *out loud* with all your heart:
> *Jesus, I know that have sinned and need Your forgiveness. I believe You died on the cross for me, and God raised You from the dead. I invite You to come into my heart to be my Lord and Savior. I want to follow you all the days of my life and spend eternity with you.*

If you prayed this prayer to receive Jesus as your Lord and Savior, You have changed your destiny and will spend eternity with God! The decision you made has changed you into a new person. You have become a child of God.

> Therefore if any man be in Christ, he is a new creature: old things are passed away; behold, all things are become new. (2 Corinthians 5:17 KJV)

If you have prayed this prayer, please contact Family Harvest Church (708-614-6000; www.fhclife.org) or a Bible believing church near you. They will provide you additional information about your new life in Jesus Christ. They will minister to any special needs or prayer requests that you have. They will assist you in finding a church in your area if you need to find one. It is important that this is not just a one-time prayer, but you follow Jesus the rest of your life and study the Word of God.

EPILOGUE

There have been modern day writings about the true birth of The Lamb of God, of which the writers may not have even been aware of the full extent of what they wrote. As God gives us this fresh understanding of His Word, He also moves upon the hearts of men to reveal more and more about His Son. Some of this revelation comes through songs. They are often written under the anointing of God, inspired by the Holy Spirit, and God's profound wisdom comes forth. These songwriters may not have even known the extent of their writings it at the time, but they obeyed the voice of the Holy Spirit by writing the words He told them to write.

WHAT CHILD IS THIS?

One example is the Christmas song "What Child Is This?" The words were written by William Chatterton Dix in 1865. It was originally written by Dix as the poem "The Manger Throne." It is set to the music of the 16th Century melody "Greensleeves," arranged by Sir John Stainer (http://www. hymnsandcarolsofchristmas. com/ Hymns_and_Carols/ what_child_is_this_version_1.htm).

Some of the words from "What Child Is This" are:

> What Child is this, who laid to rest On Mary's lap is sleeping? Whom angels greet with anthems sweet While shepherds watch are keeping?

> Refrain: *This, this is Christ the King, Whom shepherds guard* and angels sing; Haste, Haste, to bring him laud, The Babe, the Son of Mary.

Please note in the refrain that it says that the shepherds were guarding Jesus. They truly were. They "guarded" Jesus just as they would the guard Temple lambs, because the shepherds were the shepherds of the Temple flock. They needed to protect the sacrificial lambs. They knew who Jesus was because of the preparation they had with the birth of the Temple lambs. They recognized Jesus for who He was, and guarded him. This is such a profound line in this song. This is my favorite Christmas carol – and maybe that is why I recognized the revelation of this line from "What Child Is This?"

I HEARD THE BELLS ON CHRISTMAS DAY

On January 1, 2014, we were sitting in a restaurant in Branson, MO, where we have a home. The restaurant plays Christian music, and the song "I Heard the Bells on Christmas Day" by Casting Crowns was being played. I felt the presence and power of God so strong. The song was anointed and I heard it like I have never heard it before. The opening lines are:

> I heard the bells on Christmas day
> Their old familiar carols play
> And mild and sweet their songs repeat
> Of peace on earth good will to men
> And in despair I bowed my head
> There is no peace on earth I said
> For hate is strong and mocks the song
> Of peace on earth, good will to men
> Then rang the bells more loud and deep
> God is not dead, nor doth He sleep
> The wrong shall fail, the right prevail
> With peace on earth, good will to men

That evening I sought the Lord to understand the message He wanted me to know from this song. Each time I listened to that song on internet links, I could feel God's presence stronger. I played every version of it that I could find – from the Carpenters, Johnny Cash, Burl Ives and to others. There was a message in those lyrics. I knew it related to the verse of Luke 2:14: "Peace on earth; goodwill to men." Then I found a version on You

Tube that caught my attention. It was listed as the song title, plus "Civil War Background."

I played the song and it provided the explanation of the background for the writing of this song. The setting was the Christmas of 1863 during the turmoil of the Civil War. The author was Henry Wadsworth Longfellow. He sat pondering the state of life. It had been only two years since he lost his wife to a fire. His son was shot in a Civil War Battle on December 1st and he was nursing him on a long road to recovery. He heard the church bells ring out and he penned these words. When you listen to the words in the context in which it was written, it is so profound. I encourage you to watch this video link (http://www.youtube.com/watch?v=oZtNlZmnEMU). (Note: The original words of Longfellow poem are a little bit different from the ones in the current day song, but most are the same and the message and key words are identical).

I sought the Lord for more revelation on the words that became key to me "Peace on Earth; Goodwill to Men" (Luke 2:14), which I knew was the tie to the work of this book. When Jesus was born and appeared to the shepherds, the angels were praising God with those words – and those words have remained. It was a proclamation from heaven that God is with us – and He has never left this earth – and resides to this day. He will be with us until the time of the Great Tribulation – but will return when Jesus returns to earth as the King of kings and Lord of lords. Halleluiah.

God did walk in the Garden in Eden with Adam and Eve, but after they sinned and were cast out of the Garden, it was not the same. God then did appear to men and had a close relationship with them (like Enoch, Abraham and Moses), but it was not the same. Yes, His presence was in the Tabernacle and in the Temple, but it was not the same.

When Jesus was born, God came to this earth and has remained except from the time of the Ascension of Jesus until the Holy Spirit came on Pentecost. The 120 remained together in the upper room and prayed because the presence of God was not on this earth. But God returned in the person of the Holy Spirit and remains to this day. That proclamation of the angels was more than an announcement to the shepherds. It is a proclamation to all mankind. The Messiah's "peace that leads to salvation to all men of good kindly will" was given to mankind that day. Man could once again have fellowship with God Almighty. God gave us Himself.

Longfellow looked around and saw the sad state of life – the Civil War, his wife's untimely death, his son's wounding in battle and despaired. He reflected wondering how God could have sent peace on earth when there was this turmoil on earth. The answer is found in Jesus' words, recorded in John 16:33. "These things I have spoken to you, that in Me you may have peace. In the world you will have tribulation; but be of good cheer, I have overcome the world" (NKJV). The answer is that the turmoil will be around us, but we find our "peace" in Jesus and the Holy Spirit. The peace that came to the world on Christmas Day is ours today. It is up to you to accept the peace of Jesus – ask him into your heart and become His – and you will find the peace that God the Father sent to this earth. If you have not done so already, please turn to Chapter 1 in my book *The Lamb Eternal* and pray the prayer to make Jesus the Lord of your life. Then continue following after Him with all your heart.

2000 DECEMBERS AGO
A more modern day example of a God-inspired song is "2000 Decembers Ago" which is sung by Joy Williams. It was written by Joel Lindsey as part of a musical about the birth of Jesus. A line in the chorus strikes a chord profoundly. It says:

> Was anyone able to look at the stable
> And not see a child but a King...

The answer is yes – the shepherds did.

EMMANUEL
Jesus is called Emmanuel (or Immanuel depending upon the translations), meaning God with us (Isaiah 7:14; Matthew 1:23).

That turns us to one last Christmas song. It is Emmanuel, as sung by Amy Grant, Michael W. Smith, and the two of them together. Craig Smith wrote this song. The lyrics repeat and are:

Emmanuel, Emmanuel.
Wonderful, Counselor!
Lord of life, Lord of all;
He's the Prince of Peace, Mighty God, Holy One!
Emmanuel, Emmanuel.

Notice the words. Jesus is the Lord of life, the Lord of all, and the Prince of Peace. When Jesus came to earth, He became God with us, and the Prince of Peace. He is the "peace" from Longfellow's words.

BIBLIOGRAPHY

Abrams, Cooper. *Where was the Birth Place of our Lord Jesus?* Bible Truth. bibletruth.org

Blankschaen, Bill. *Was Jesus born away in a manger?* Faithwalkers. http://www.patheos.com/blogs/faithwalkers/2012/12/was-jesus-born-away-in-a-manger-at-migdal-eder. Accessed 3-8-17

Christian Classics Ethereal Library. *Alfred Edersheim.* Grand Rapids, MI: ccel.org

Coffman, Elesha. *Why December 25th?* Christianity Today. christianitytoday.com, 2008, accessed March 18, 2017

Custodia Terrae Sanctae. www.custodia.org

Dake, Finis Jennings. *Dake's Annotated Reference Bible.* Lawrenceville, Georgia: Dake Bible Sales, Inc., 1991.

Dix, William Chatterton. *What Child Is This?* 1865. Hymns and Carols of Christmas. http://www. hymnsandcarolsofchristmas.com

Duran, Jacob. *This Shall Be a Sign* http://letterstotheflock.blogspot.com/2007/12/this-shall-be-sign. html

Dyer, Dr. Charles. *Shepherds: More Than Field Hands*. Land and the Book Radio. Moody Bible Radio. www.thelandandthebook.org.

Edersheim, Alfred. *The Life and Times of Jesus the Messiah*. Grand Rapids, MI: http://www.ccel.org/ccel/edersheim/lifetimes.html. accessed 3-14-17.

Edwards, Gene. *A Tale of Three Kings*. Carol Stream, IL: Tyndale House Publishers. 1992.

Eusebius Pamphili. *Church History, Church History, the Life of Constantine, Oration in Praise*. http://www.ccel.org/ccel/schaff/npnf201.iv.vi.iii.xliii.html accessed 4-27-17

Freeman, James M. *The New Manners and Customs of the Bible*. Alachua, FL: Bridge-Logos Publishers. 1998.

Henry, Matthew. *Matthew Henry's Concise Commentary on the Whole Bible*. Bible Gatweay.com (http://www.biblegateway.com/resources/matthew-henry/Mic.4.8-Mic.4.13)

Hickey, Marilyn. *Jesus In Every Book Of The Bible*. Englewood, CO: Marilyn Ministries. 2009.

Howard, Kevin and Rosenthal, Marvin. *The Feasts of the Lord*. Nashville, TN: Thomas Nelson, Inc., 1997.

Norton, Michael. *The Lamb, Yahweh*. Faithgateway.com. 2015. http://www.faithgateway.com/lamb-yahweh/#.WXaHJ4jyuT8

Origen. *Contra Celsum*, Book 1, Chapter 51. Accessed from http://www.newadvent.org/fathers/04161.htm 4-27-17.

Pixner, Bargil. *Fifth Gospel*. Rosh Pina, Israel: Corazin Publishing, 1992.

Schiel, Skip. *Walk Jerusalem to Bethlehem*. Teeksa Photography. 2007. https://skipschiel.wordpress.com/2007/12/25/walk-jerusalem -to-bethlehem/

See The Holy Land. *St. Jerome's Cave*. http://www.seetheholyland. net/st-jerome's-cave

Short, Rabbi Mike L. *Migdal Eder*. Mayhim Hayhim Ministries.

Accessed from http://www.mayimhayim.org.

Smith, haRold. *The Birth – Revisited*. He That Has An Ear. *http://hethathasanear.com/Birth.html*.

The Mishnah. http://www.sefaria.org